THE PERFUME WARS

Scent Trade Rivalries That Toppled Provincial Governors

Drusilla Nightham

This book is a work of nonfiction. It draws on published historical, journalistic, and scholarly sources, and every effort has been made to ensure factual accuracy at the time of writing. Where source material is incomplete or contested, this has been noted in the text rather than resolved through speculation.

Contents

Introduction

A smell has never started a war on its own. No general has ever marched an army because a rival kingdom's rose fields smelled sweeter than his own. And yet, across five thousand years of recorded human commerce, the specific, narrow, geographically stubborn business of extracting fragrance from flowers, wood, resin, and animal glands has toppled governors, funded rebellions, sustained a thirty year guerrilla war in the forests of southern India, triggered a genocide on a cluster of volcanic islands in the Indonesian archipelago, and quietly shaped the tax policy of empires that no longer exist. This book is an attempt to take that pattern seriously, to follow it from the tanneries of sixteenth century Provence to the fermentation vats of twenty first century Swiss biotechnology laboratories, and to ask, at every stop along the way, the same simple question. Who controlled the source, and what did that control actually cost the people who lived near it.

The answer, chapter after chapter, turns out to be strikingly consistent. A fragrant material grows, or forms, or washes ashore, in one place and nowhere else in any commercially meaningful quantity. Whoever controls that place, a royal decree, a colonial trading company, a guild charter, a state forest department, gains leverage over a much larger territory than the growing region itself, leverage that provincial administrators, however powerful they might otherwise appear, have repeatedly found themselves unable to fully resist. This is not a book about perfume in the sense of top notes and base notes, sillage and longevity, the vocabulary a fragrance reviewer might use to describe a new release. It is a book about the specific, often brutal economics of scarcity, and about the ordinary people, farmers, forest rangers, harvesters, smugglers, whose lives were shaped by decisions made, in most cases, centuries before they were born.

Twelve chapters follow, moving roughly chronologically and geographically, from the glove workshops of Grasse through the royal forests of Mysore, the volcanic Banda Islands, the Bulgarian Rose Valley, the high alpine range of the Himalaya, the ancient resin coast of Somaliland, and finally into the chemistry laboratories and fermentation vats that have spent the last century and a half trying, with only partial success, to make every one of these conflicts obsolete. Every figure, date, and statistic in the pages that follow comes from documented historical and contemporary record. Where the underlying facts are genuinely contested or incomplete, this book says so plainly rather than filling the gap with invention. The story does not need embellishment. It has never needed embellishment. It only needed, until now, someone willing to follow the smell all the way back to its source.

CHAPTER ONE

The Reek That Built an Empire

There is a particular kind of irony that history seems to enjoy more than any novelist would dare invent, and it sits quietly at the center of the town of Grasse. For four hundred years this small settlement in the hills above Cannes has worn the title of perfume capital of the world, a place where the air itself is said to carry the scent of jasmine and rose from May through October, where the biggest fashion houses on earth still come to buy their raw materials, and where a schoolchild can point out the difference between an absolute and an essential oil before she can multiply fractions. And yet Grasse did not become the perfume capital of the world because someone there loved beautiful smells. Grasse became the perfume capital of the world because the people who lived there, for centuries, could not stand the smell of themselves.

Until the sixteenth century, Grasse was known across Europe for one thing only, and that thing was leather. The town sat in a fold of hills that gave it access to water, to hides, and to the particular combination of tannins and oak bark that made for excellent tanning conditions, and its tanneries turned out gloves, purses, and harnesses that were shipped across the continent. But tanning, as anyone who has stood downwind of a working tannery can attest, is one of the most aggressively unpleasant industrial processes ever devised by human beings. The hides had to be soaked in lime to loosen the hair, scraped, then soaked again in vats that in the sixteenth century commonly used dog feces and animal brains to soften the leather through a process called bating, before finally being cured in tannin baths made from crushed oak bark steeped in water for months. The stench did not stay politely inside the tannery walls. It settled into the stone of the town, into the clothes of the workers, into the well water, into the reputation of Grasse itself, a reputation that traveling merchants carried with them to every market they visited.

The nobility of France, who prized their leather gloves as a mark of refinement, found themselves in an uncomfortable bind. They wanted the fine, supple gloves that Grasse tanners produced, gloves soft enough to be pulled over a lady's fingers without catching on a single ring, but they did not want their hands to smell of lime and dog dung for the rest of the afternoon. Sometime in the middle of the sixteenth century, a Grasse glovemaker named Galimard hit on the solution. He began macerating flowers, jasmine and lavender picked from the surrounding hillsides, in animal fat, and using the resulting scented pomade to dress the finished gloves. The stench of the tanning did not disappear, but it was masked, buried under something a customer would actually want pressed against her skin.

This single decision, made by a craftsman trying to sell more gloves rather than by any visionary trying to build an industry, is the actual founding act of the modern perfume trade as the world understands it. It is worth sitting with that for a moment, because it undercuts almost every romantic myth that perfume houses like to tell about themselves today, myths involving ancient wisdom and mystical noses passed down through generations. The truth is blunter and, in its own way, more interesting. Perfume was invented in Grasse as a commercial patch, a way of covering up a manufacturing defect so a product could be sold to customers who would otherwise have refused to touch it. The entire aesthetic industry that would later produce Chanel No. 5, Shalimar, and Joy did not begin with an artist chasing beauty. It began with a businessman chasing a sale.

The story gained its most famous, if not entirely verifiable, embellishment through Catherine de Medici, the Italian noblewoman who became queen of France in 1547 through her marriage to Henry the Second. Catherine had grown up in Florence, a city with its own tradition of perfumed leather goods, and she is widely credited, in Grasse's own civic memory if not always in strict archival documentation, with popularizing scented gloves at the French court after receiving a pair crafted in the Grasse style. Whether Catherine herself was the decisive tastemaker or simply one prominent early adopter among several, the effect on Grasse's fortunes was the same. Once scented gloves became fashionable among the French aristocracy, demand for the flowers used to scent them exploded, and the hillsides around Grasse, which had a mild Mediterranean microclimate uncommonly well suited to growing delicate flowering plants, began filling with fields of jasmine, rose, and lavender.

What followed over the next century and a half was not a single dramatic event but something closer to a slow-motion economic coup, one industry quietly strangling another within the same town walls. As demand for scented leather grew, more and more of Grasse's agricultural land was converted from grain and olives to flowers, a shift that historians of the region note began accelerating through the 1600s as the perfume trade proved more profitable per hectare than traditional farming. By 1724, the glovemakers and perfumers of Grasse had organized themselves into a single professional guild, the Guild of Glovers and Perfumers, formally recognized by the French crown, a document that marked the moment the scent business stopped being an accessory to leather and became powerful enough to negotiate its own legal standing. It is a small thing on paper, a guild charter, but guild charters in early modern France were instruments of real economic control. They determined who could legally practice a trade, who could train apprentices, who could sell finished goods within a jurisdiction, and who could be excluded. Grasse's perfumers, in winning their own guild status, had won the right to police their own industry, which meant they had won the right to decide who got rich from it.

Then, in 1789, a tax on leather imposed as part of the broader fiscal crisis that would soon help topple the French monarchy altogether made the tanning side of Grasse's economy suddenly far less profitable. Tanners across the region began closing their operations or shifting their capital elsewhere. The perfumers, whose raw material was flowers grown in French soil rather than imported hides subject to new duties, felt none of the same pressure. Within a generation, the industry that had begun as a cosmetic afterthought to leather had become the dominant economic force in the town, and the tanneries that had given Grasse its original reputation, and its original stench, had all but vanished. The child industry had eaten its parent.

None of this happened without conflict, and it is here that the story of Grasse begins to earn its place in a book about wars rather than a book about pleasant flowers. The land around Grasse suitable for growing jasmine and rose at commercial scale was not infinite, and as the perfume trade grew, competition over the best plots intensified sharply. Local seigneurial landholders, the minor nobility who controlled much of the surrounding countryside under the feudal land arrangements that persisted in provincial France well into the eighteenth century, found themselves sitting on assets that had suddenly become extraordinarily valuable. Land that had rented for a modest sum as ordinary farmland could command dramatically higher rates once a perfumer had proven it could support commercial jasmine cultivation, and disputes over lease terms, over water rights for irrigation, and over the boundaries of parcels became a recurring feature of local court records through the eighteenth and nineteenth centuries.

The flowers themselves imposed a brutal seasonal logic on all of this that made the stakes even higher. Jasmine has to be picked before dawn, while the blossoms are still closed and their volatile oils have not yet begun evaporating in the morning heat, which meant that during the harvest season, roughly from August through October, entire villages emptied into the fields before sunrise, picking by hand, moving fast, because a delay of even a few hours could measurably reduce the oil yield of the crop. Rose behaved similarly, with the traditional harvest window in the Grasse region running through May and closing quickly as temperatures rose. This was not a crop that tolerated labor disputes or logistical hiccups. A grower who could not get enough pickers into his fields during the narrow window of peak bloom could lose the better part of a year's income in a matter of days, and this vulnerability gave enormous leverage to whoever controlled labor, water, and access to processing facilities during those critical weeks.

By the nineteenth century, the perfume houses of Grasse, family firms like Chiris, Molinard, and later

Fragonard, had grown large enough and wealthy enough to function as something closer to regional economic powers than simple manufacturers, and their influence over the surrounding countryside began to resemble, in miniature, the kind of soft political control that agricultural monopolies have exerted in other parts of the world before and since. The houses did not merely buy flowers on the open market. Many entered into exclusive, multiyear contracts with growers, locking in supply and price in exchange for guaranteed purchase, a system that stabilized the industry but also meant that a handful of firms in Grasse effectively set the economic terms under which thousands of small farming families across the surrounding hills would live. When the houses prospered, the growers prospered. When the houses cut prices, entire villages felt it.

This concentration of economic power did not go unnoticed by the administrative authorities who governed the region on behalf of Paris. Provincial administrators, first under the old regime as intendants and later, after the Revolution, as prefects and sub prefects of the department of Alpes Maritimes, were tasked with maintaining order and tax revenue across territories that included Grasse, and the perfume trade complicated that job considerably. A single bad harvest, a price collapse imposed by the Grasse houses, or a dispute between rival perfumers over access to a prized field could ripple outward into local unrest that provincial officials were expected to contain. Local administrative correspondence from the department through the nineteenth century repeatedly references disputes tied to the flower trade, ranging from disagreements over communal irrigation channels feeding the flower fields to conflicts between rival buyers attempting to secure exclusive access to a grower's harvest before a competitor could reach the same farmer.

The perfume houses, for their part, learned quickly that political relationships mattered as much as horticultural ones. Securing favorable tax treatment, protecting the department's flower exports from disadvantageous trade agreements negotiated in Paris, and ensuring that infrastructure investment, particularly the roads and later railways needed to move both fresh flowers and finished perfume to market, favored Grasse over competing regions required sustained lobbying of exactly the kind of provincial administrators who nominally oversaw the industry rather than served it. Grasse's perfumers cultivated relationships with sub prefects and departmental councilors with the same patience and attention they brought to cultivating jasmine, understanding that an unfavorable administrator, one who prioritized a rival industry, imposed unwelcome taxes, or simply failed to advocate for Grasse's interests in Paris, could do more damage to the trade in a single budget cycle than a poor harvest could in a full season.

It would be an exaggeration bordering on fiction to claim that the perfumers of Grasse personally toppled provincial governors the way a palace coup topples a monarch. French provincial administration in the eighteenth and nineteenth centuries did not typically end in dramatic depositions of the kind associated with royal courts or colonial territories. But it is not an exaggeration to say that Grasse's scent trade became, over the course of two centuries, powerful enough to make or break the political fortunes of the men sent to administer the region, powerful enough that an administrator who crossed the perfume houses risked seeing his tenure cut short through the quieter mechanisms available in French provincial politics: unfavorable reports sent to Paris by well connected merchants, withdrawn support in local elections after French administrative reforms introduced elected councils, and a business community capable of making an official's daily governance simply much harder than it needed to be. The perfumers of Grasse did not need muskets or mobs. They had something more durable in provincial French politics: money, patience, and the kind of multigenerational local roots that outlasted any single administrator's term.

Consider the case of the flower tax disputes of the 1850s and 1860s, a period well documented in regional archival material, during which the perfume houses of Grasse organized sustained opposition to proposed increases in local taxation intended to fund departmental infrastructure projects that the houses considered wasteful or, worse, beneficial to rival towns rather than to

Grasse itself. The perfumers argued, with some justification, that their industry already generated substantial tax revenue through the export of finished perfume and that further levies on the raw flower trade would simply push growers to abandon cultivation in favor of less heavily taxed crops, undermining the very tax base the administration hoped to expand. Provincial officials who pushed too aggressively for the new levies found their proposals stalled, amended beyond recognition, or quietly shelved after sustained pressure from a coalition of growers and perfume house owners who understood, correctly, that their collective economic weight in the local economy gave them influence that individual farmers in other trades simply did not possess.

What makes Grasse's story genuinely remarkable, and worth the opening chapter of a book about scent trade rivalries, is not any single dramatic confrontation but the sheer durability of the pattern it established. Nearly every conflict examined in the chapters that follow, the sandalwood monopolies of Mysore, the rose oil taxation battles of Ottoman Bulgaria, the ambergris smuggling networks that operate today exactly as they did four centuries ago, the frankincense trade of the Somali coast, follows a structural logic first perfected, if not invented, in the hills above Cannes. A fragrant raw material grows in a specific, geographically constrained place. Whoever controls access to that place, whether through land ownership, royal decree, or simple market consolidation, gains outsized economic and political leverage over a much larger territory than the growing region itself. And the administrators nominally responsible for governing that territory find themselves, again and again, having to choose between the interests of the scent trade and their own political survival.

By the twentieth century, Grasse's perfumers had formalized their influence into institutions that outlasted any individual administrator's career. The Chambre de Commerce et d'Industrie de Grasse, established to represent the collective interests of the town's businesses, became a permanent lobbying force in regional politics, one that no provincial official could realistically ignore for long. When the international vanilla and synthetic fragrance markets began threatening the natural flower trade in the early twentieth century, it was this institutional structure, decades in the building, that allowed Grasse to pivot, lobby for protective designations, and ultimately secure the kind of geographic branding protection that today allows growers in the region to market their jasmine and rose as authentically Grasse in a global marketplace flooded with cheaper synthetic and imported alternatives.

The town's flowers still bloom on the same hillsides that Galimard's sixteenth century contemporaries first planted to cover the smell of their tanneries, though far fewer hectares are under cultivation today than at the industry's nineteenth century peak, when thousands of tons of jasmine and rose petals were processed annually. Today only a few dozen tons of raw flower material move through Grasse each season, a fraction of the historical volume, as global fragrance houses increasingly source cheaper jasmine from Egypt and India and turn to synthetic reproductions of natural scent molecules that can be manufactured in a laboratory for a tiny fraction of the cost of hand harvested petals. But the political and economic lessons Grasse taught the world about the leverage embedded in scarce, geographically fixed fragrant materials would echo across five continents and four centuries, in kingdoms and colonies its original glovemakers never knew existed, wherever a rare and beautiful smell turned out to be worth fighting, taxing, smuggling, or dying for.

That is where this book goes next: eastward and southward, out of the gentle hills of Provence and into the royal forests of Mysore, where a very different ruler was about to discover that the smell of sandalwood could be worth more than gold, and that declaring a tree the property of the crown was a great deal easier than actually keeping it there.

CHAPTER TWO

The Royal Tree

In 1792, a ruler under enormous military pressure from the most powerful colonial force on earth made a decision that had nothing directly to do with soldiers, cannons, or treaties, and everything to do with a slow growing, fragrant tree. Tipu Sultan, ruler of the Kingdom of Mysore in southern India, had just concluded the Third Anglo Mysore War with the British East India Company on unfavorable terms, ceding roughly half his territory and paying a crushing war indemnity. He needed revenue, and he needed it in a form that could not easily be seized, taxed away, or bargained out of him at the negotiating table. He looked at the sandalwood forests within his remaining domain and declared Santalum album, the sandalwood tree, a Royal Tree, the property of the state regardless of whose land it grew on. It was one of the earliest and most consequential natural resource monopolies in modern history, and it would outlive the man who created it by more than two centuries.

To understand why Tipu Sultan reached for sandalwood specifically, it helps to understand what the wood actually was worth, and to whom. Santalum album, native to the hill forests of southern India, produces a heartwood saturated with fragrant oils, chiefly a compound class called santalols, that give it a warm, creamy, almost buttery scent unlike any other wood on earth. Unlike most aromatic materials, sandalwood's fragrance does not fade quickly. Carved into religious statuary, ground into paste for ceremonial use, or distilled into oil, sandalwood retains its scent for years, sometimes decades, which made it uniquely valuable across a range of markets that had almost nothing else in common with each other. Hindu temples across India used sandalwood paste in daily ritual. Buddhist monasteries throughout East and Southeast Asia burned sandalwood incense as a central part of religious practice. Chinese buyers, in particular, developed an enormous and sustained appetite for sandalwood imports for use in incense, medicine, and fine furniture, an appetite that predated Tipu Sultan's reign by centuries and that would continue to drive the sandalwood trade long after his kingdom had ceased to exist as an independent state.

A single mature sandalwood tree takes between thirty and sixty years to develop commercially valuable heartwood, a timeline that immediately separates sandalwood from almost every other commodity discussed in this book. Jasmine can be replanted and harvested within a single growing season. Rose bushes reach productive maturity within a few years. Sandalwood, by contrast, operates on something closer to a human generational timescale. A ruler who controlled sandalwood forests in 1792 was not simply managing an annual harvest. He was managing an asset whose supply could not be meaningfully expanded within his own lifetime, no matter how much capital or labor he threw at the problem, because the trees planted today would not be ready for harvest until his grandchildren's era. This biological reality is what transformed sandalwood from a valuable commodity into something closer to a strategic reserve, comparable in some ways to a mineral deposit, and it is precisely this scarcity, this inability to simply grow more supply on demand, that made state control over existing forests so attractive to a ruler in Tipu Sultan's position.

Tipu Sultan was, by most historical accounts, an unusually sophisticated economic administrator for his time and place, and his sandalwood monopoly did not exist in isolation. He extended similar state control over a range of other valuable commodities within his kingdom, including pepper, cardamom, elephants, and timber more broadly, establishing dozens of state factories to process and export these goods under royal supervision. This was not simple confiscation for its own sake. Tipu Sultan understood that in an era when European trading companies were rapidly expanding their commercial and military footprint across India, a ruler without a well organized, centrally controlled revenue base capable of funding an army and a modern administration would not survive contact with the British East India Company for long. Sandalwood, precisely because of its long maturation cycle and its consistent international demand, offered something close to a guaranteed, renewable revenue stream, provided the state could actually enforce its claim over the forests where the trees grew.

Enforcement, as it turned out, was the entire problem, and it would remain the entire problem for the next two hundred and thirty years. Declaring a tree the property of the crown on paper was straightforward. Preventing individual farmers, local landholders, and organized smuggling networks from cutting down trees growing on land they considered their own, or on remote forest tracts far from any government outpost, required a level of continuous administrative and military presence that no government controlling this territory, whether Tipu Sultan's own kingdom, the East India Company that succeeded him, the British Raj that followed the Company, or independent India's Karnataka state government after 1947, ever fully achieved. The gap between the law on paper and the reality on the ground became, over two centuries, one of the most persistent and violent resource conflicts in South Asian history.

Tipu Sultan died in battle in 1799, killed defending his capital at Seringapatam during the Fourth Anglo Mysore War, and his kingdom passed under British colonial control, restored in reduced form to the Wadiyar dynasty that had ruled Mysore before Tipu Sultan's father seized power decades earlier, but now operating as what colonial administrators called a princely state, nominally sovereign but firmly subordinate to British political authority. What is genuinely striking, and historically significant, is what the British chose to do with Tipu Sultan's sandalwood monopoly once they held effective control over the territory. Rather than dismantling a state monopoly that a defeated Muslim ruler had personally instituted, largely as a wartime revenue measure against them, the British colonial administration kept it. The revenue potential was simply too attractive to abandon on ideological grounds. State owned sandalwood warehouses, known locally as sandal koti, continued operating under British oversight, and the principle that sandalwood belonged to the state regardless of whose land it grew on survived the transition from independent kingdom to colonial protectorate almost entirely intact.

This continuity across radically different political regimes is worth pausing on, because it reveals something important about how resource monopolies function once they become institutionally entrenched. The British East India Company had no particular ideological attachment to Tipu Sultan's economic philosophy, and in most respects the Company actively dismantled or restructured the administrative systems it inherited from defeated Indian rulers. But sandalwood revenue was sandalwood revenue, and a colonial administration under constant pressure to make its Indian territories self funding was not about to walk away from a reliable income stream simply because a defeated enemy had set it up first. The monopoly outlived its creator's dynasty, outlived the specific political circumstances of the 1790s that had motivated its creation, and settled into something closer to a permanent feature of the regional economy, one that successive governments would maintain less because they agreed with the underlying logic and more because dismantling it seemed riskier than keeping it running.

Through the nineteenth and into the twentieth century, sandalwood remained a major revenue source for the Mysore state, later princely state, under continued Wadiyar rule with British political oversight, contributing an estimated average share of the kingdom's total revenue that made it one of the most economically significant single commodities the state controlled. In 1916, the Mysore government established a dedicated sandalwood oil distillery, formalizing what had previously been a more scattered and informal processing system into an integrated state enterprise that controlled the trade from forest to finished product, extracting oil directly rather than simply exporting raw logs and ceding the more profitable processing stage to foreign buyers. This vertical integration, keeping the entire value chain within state control, represented a significant sophistication of the original monopoly model and reflected a growing understanding, among Mysore's administrators, that the real money in sandalwood lay not in the raw wood itself but in the distilled oil, a far more valuable and easily transported product that commanded premium prices in international perfumery, medicine, and religious markets.

The twentieth century brought a new complication that Tipu Sultan, focused on the immediate military and fiscal pressures of the 1790s, could not have anticipated: the actual sustainability of the resource itself. As international demand for sandalwood oil grew, particularly from the expanding global fragrance and cosmetics industries centered in Europe and increasingly in the United States, pressure on Karnataka's remaining wild sandalwood forests intensified sharply, even as the state monopoly nominally restricting harvest remained in place. By the late twentieth century, the strain was becoming impossible to ignore in the production statistics themselves. Legal, state authorized sandalwood production in Karnataka collapsed from roughly three thousand tonnes annually in 1978 to a mere twenty tonnes by 2002, a decline of more than ninety nine percent in under twenty five years, a statistic so severe that the International Union for Conservation of Nature classified Santalum album as a vulnerable species by 1997.

This collapse was not primarily the result of legal, state sanctioned harvesting outpacing the forest's regenerative capacity, though decades of continuous extraction certainly played a role. The more significant driver, and the one that transformed the Mysore sandalwood story from a simple case of resource depletion into a genuine, decades long war fought with automatic weapons and landmines, was the widening gap between the artificially low prices the Karnataka state forest department paid its own licensed processing factories for raw sandalwood, and the astronomical prices the same wood could command on illegal international markets. The state, in effect, created the very smuggling economy that would eventually devastate its own forests, by maintaining a monopoly pricing structure so far below true market value that organized criminal networks could offer forest dwelling communities and corrupt local officials sums of money the legal system simply could not match.

Into this gap stepped Koose Munisamy Veerappan, the single most notorious figure in the entire history of the Mysore sandalwood trade, and a man whose three and a half decade career as a forest bandit turned the state's fragrant monopoly into one of the bloodiest resource conflicts in modern Indian history. Veerappan operated in the dense forest terrain where the borders of Karnataka, Tamil Nadu, and Kerala converge, a landscape of genuine wilderness that gave him and his network natural cover against the state forces sent to stop him. Over the course of his career, Veerappan's gang is estimated to have smuggled roughly sixty five tonnes of sandalwood, along with substantial quantities of poached ivory, worth a combined total of approximately twenty two million dollars, an extraordinary sum extracted from state owned forests over more than three decades of sustained, low level warfare against Indian state authority.

The human cost of this conflict separates it decisively from the more familiar white collar crime narratives that usually accompany stories of smuggling and black markets. Veerappan's operation is credited with killing approximately one hundred and eighty four people over the course of his career, roughly half of them police officers and forest department rangers sent to apprehend him, a casualty count that places the Mysore sandalwood conflict closer to a genuine, if geographically confined, insurgency than to conventional organized crime. Indian state authorities responded in kind. Successive Karnataka and Tamil Nadu governments deployed dedicated Special Task Forces, essentially paramilitary units created for the specific purpose of hunting Veerappan and dismantling his network, and the resulting conflict dragged on for the better part of two decades before Veerappan was finally killed in an ambush by the Tamil Nadu Special Task Force in October 2004, ending one of the longest sustained manhunts in the history of South Asian law enforcement.

What makes Veerappan's story genuinely important to a book about scent trade wars, rather than simply a colorful footnote in Indian criminal history, is the direct line that connects his violence to the specific economic architecture Tipu Sultan established more than two centuries earlier. The core structural problem was never really about Veerappan as an individual. It was about a state monopoly system that criminalized the harvest of a naturally growing tree species regardless of the harvester's actual land ownership, while simultaneously paying licensed producers prices so far below international market value that an enormous financial incentive for illegal harvesting was baked directly into the system's own design. Successive governments understood this dynamic and largely chose to maintain it anyway, because the alternative, genuine market liberalization that might have allowed private cultivation and competitive pricing, threatened the state's own revenue capture from its remaining processing monopoly.

The state's continued mismanagement of this dynamic, even after Veerappan's death removed the most visible symbol of the conflict, remained a documented feature of Karnataka sandalwood policy well into the twenty first century. The Karnataka Forest Department continued selling harvested sandalwood to its state owned processing factories at artificially depressed prices even as illegal harvesting continued to devastate remaining wild populations, while simultaneously shifting the practical burden of tree protection onto private landowners, who faced heavy fines and significant jail time if sandalwood trees growing on their own property were stolen or damaged, a legal arrangement that effectively asked private citizens to bear the risk and liability of guarding a state owned asset they were not permitted to profit from themselves. This combination, harsh penalties for private citizens whose trees were stolen, combined with a state pricing structure that made legal sale unattractive relative to illegal smuggling, created exactly the kind of perverse incentive structure that sustained the black market Veerappan and countless smaller operators exploited for generations.

Private cultivation of sandalwood was finally legalized in the Indian state framework in 2001, a policy shift that came only after decades of forest collapse had made the unsustainability of the pure state monopoly model impossible to ignore any longer, and even this reform arrived too late to reverse the underlying biological reality that had shaped the entire conflict from the beginning. Sandalwood takes thirty years or more to mature into commercially harvestable heartwood. Trees planted following the 2001 legal reforms will not reach full productive maturity until well into the 2030s at the earliest, which means that even the most well intentioned modern policy correction cannot undo, within any single generation's lifetime, the damage inflicted by more than two centuries of a state monopoly system that consistently prioritized short term revenue extraction and administrative control over long term forest sustainability.

Today, remarkably, the underlying legal and economic structure Tipu Sultan established in 1792 remains substantially intact in Karnataka.

Sandalwood growing on private land in the state can still, in significant respects, remain subject to state regulatory claims, an arrangement of genuinely startling institutional durability that has now survived the fall of Tipu Sultan's kingdom, the establishment and dissolution of the British Raj, Indian independence, the linguistic reorganization of Indian states that created modern Karnataka, and the deaths of well over a hundred people in direct violent conflict over the resource it governs. Karnataka Soaps and Detergents Limited, the state owned entity descended directly from the original royal sandalwood processing enterprise and best known today for manufacturing Mysore Sandal Soap, remains a significant commercial operation, reporting dividend payments exceeding twelve million dollars in a single recent year, proof that the underlying commodity, whatever the human and ecological cost of controlling it, has never stopped being worth fighting over.

The lesson Mysore offers, and it is a considerably darker lesson than the one Grasse taught in the previous chapter, is that state control over a scarce, slow growing, fragrant natural resource does not simply create political leverage over provincial administrators. Left unmanaged for long enough, and priced badly enough relative to genuine market value, it can create the underlying economic conditions for sustained, lethal violence, conditions that persist for generations after the original ruler who declared the monopoly is gone, and that no single subsequent government, however well intentioned its individual reforms, has yet managed to fully resolve. The tree Tipu Sultan called royal in 1792 is still, in important legal respects, the property of a state he has been dead for over two centuries. The forests that grow it are still being fought over. And the pattern he set in motion, declare the resource state property, underprice it relative to what smugglers will pay, and then police the resulting gap with escalating force, would echo, with grim consistency, in fragrant trades on nearly every continent examined in the pages that follow.

CHAPTER THREE

The Bandit of the Sandal Forests

Koose Munisamy Veerappan was born in 1952 in the village of Gopinatham, a small settlement in the forested border country where the states of Karnataka and Tamil Nadu meet along the Cauvery River, a region so remote and so densely forested that Indian state authority had only ever exerted partial, intermittent control over it, even under the relatively centralized administrative systems of British colonial rule. It is worth dwelling on this geography before turning to the man himself, because the terrain explains almost as much about the length and brutality of his career as anything about his personal character. The forests straddling the Karnataka, Tamil Nadu, and Kerala borders form one of the largest contiguous stretches of dense tropical forest remaining in peninsular India, cut through with ravines, seasonal rivers, and hill ranges that made conventional policing, the kind involving vehicles, radio communication, and rapid troop movement, extraordinarily difficult even by the standards of rural Indian law enforcement in the second half of the twentieth century.

By the account most consistently repeated in Indian law enforcement and journalistic sources, Veerappan began his criminal career as an elephant poacher in his teenage years, working within a local tradition of forest banditry that predated him by generations, in a region where sandalwood theft and ivory poaching had long coexisted as parallel, often overlapping criminal economies. What distinguished Veerappan from the numerous smaller scale poachers and smugglers who operated in the same forests was less any single innovation in method than a combination of physical toughness, genuine intimate knowledge of an exceptionally difficult terrain, and a willingness to escalate to lethal violence against law enforcement that set him apart from the general run of forest criminals the Karnataka and Tamil Nadu authorities were more accustomed to handling. Over the following decades he built, expanded, armed, and repeatedly rebuilt a gang that combined ivory poaching with the far more lucrative business of illegal sandalwood harvesting and export, exploiting exactly the pricing gap described in the previous chapter, the enormous distance between the artificially low prices Karnataka's state processing factories paid for legally sourced wood, and the far higher prices smuggled sandalwood could command once it reached buyers willing to purchase outside official channels.

The financial scale of Veerappan's operation, even accounting for the inherent difficulty of putting precise figures on any black market enterprise, was staggering by the standards of rural Indian crime. Across his career, his network is estimated to have moved approximately sixty five tonnes of illegally harvested sandalwood, together with substantial quantities of poached ivory, generating a combined market value of roughly twenty two million dollars, wealth extracted almost entirely from state owned forest land that Veerappan and his associates had no legal claim to whatsoever. This was not the operation of a lone bandit living hand to mouth in the forest. It was, in every meaningful economic sense, an organized enterprise, with its own supply chains reaching from the point of illegal harvest deep in the forest interior to buyers and processing intermediaries who moved the material into legitimate seeming commercial channels, at which point smuggled sandalwood became functionally indistinguishable from the legally sourced product moving through Karnataka's own state factories.

What transformed Veerappan from a criminal, however successful, into something closer to a genuine insurgent figure in the eyes of Indian state authority was the systematic and sustained violence his network directed against the officials sent to stop him. Across more than three decades of activity, Veerappan's gang is credited with the deaths of approximately one hundred and eighty four people, and critically, roughly half of these victims were police officers and forest department rangers, the specific state personnel tasked with enforcing the sandalwood monopoly and protecting the forests it claimed to govern. This is a casualty figure that decisively separates the Veerappan case from ordinary smuggling or poaching crime. A conventional smuggler seeks to avoid confrontation with the state, to move goods quietly and profit without drawing attention. Veerappan, over the course of a career spanning three decades, repeatedly chose direct, lethal confrontation with the specific arms of the state responsible for protecting the resource he was stealing, a pattern of behavior that eventually forced Indian authorities to treat the situation less as a law enforcement problem and more as a low intensity internal security crisis requiring paramilitary rather than conventional police response.

The scale of the state's eventual response reflected this shift in classification. Both the Karnataka and Tamil Nadu state governments, recognizing that conventional police units were poorly equipped and inadequately trained to operate effectively in the dense forest terrain Veerappan called home, established dedicated Special Task Forces, specialized paramilitary units created for the specific purpose of locating, containing, and ultimately neutralizing his network. These were not routine police postings. Officers assigned to the Special Task Forces operated for extended periods deep in forest terrain, cut off from normal urban policing infrastructure, engaged in what amounted to a jungle counterinsurgency campaign against an adversary who knew the terrain infinitely better than they did and who had, over decades of operation, built local support networks, whether through genuine loyalty, fear, or simple economic dependency on the income Veerappan's smuggling operation generated for forest dwelling communities that otherwise had few economic opportunities available to them.

The manhunt for Veerappan stretched across more than two decades and became, in its own grim way, one of the defining internal security narratives of late twentieth century India, generating sustained national media attention, political controversy over the conduct and cost of the pursuit, and periodic public debate over whether the resources devoted to hunting a single individual, however violent his record, were proportionate to the underlying problem. Veerappan repeatedly evaded capture through a combination of superior local knowledge, an extensive network of informants and sympathizers within forest communities, and, according to numerous journalistic and law enforcement accounts, periodic complicity or negligence among some local officials, whether through corruption, intimidation, or simple fear of retaliation. His ability to survive and continue operating for so long against the sustained, dedicated efforts of two separate state paramilitary forces speaks to just how deeply the underlying economic conditions that sustained his operation, the pricing gap between legal and illegal sandalwood, the poverty of forest dwelling communities with few alternative sources of income, and the practical difficulty of policing dense forest terrain, were embedded in the region's political economy rather than being simply a matter of one criminal's individual cunning.

The endgame arrived in October 2004, when the Tamil Nadu Special Task Force, after years of accumulated intelligence and repeated near misses, finally located and killed Veerappan in an ambush, ending a manhunt that had by then become something close to a national obsession, covered extensively across Indian media for the better part of two decades. Photographs released by Indian authorities following the operation showed his body, wrapped in cloth with only his face visible, his once iconic handlebar moustache cut away, images that were widely understood within India as a deliberate demonstration of the state's authority finally reasserted over a figure who had, for so long, appeared to operate beyond its reach. The message conveyed, quite explicitly, was that summary and final justice awaited anyone who defied state sandalwood authority with the sustained violence Veerappan had employed for more than thirty years.

But Veerappan's death, however dramatic its staging and however genuinely it closed one specific chapter of violence, did not resolve the underlying structural conflict that had produced him in the first place, and this is the point at which his individual story connects back to the larger argument this book is making about scent trade wars more broadly. The core problem was never Veerappan as a singular criminal mastermind. It was a state monopoly system, inherited with remarkably little modification from Tipu Sultan's eighteenth century decree, that continued paying licensed sandalwood producers prices dramatically below the wood's actual international market value, while simultaneously criminalizing the harvest of trees that, in an economically rational system, private landowners and forest dwelling communities might have had genuine incentive to cultivate, protect, and sell through legal channels rather than illegal ones. As long as that fundamental pricing gap persisted, the economic incentive for someone to fill the role Veerappan had occupied would persist alongside it, whatever became of the man himself.

Indeed, the years following Veerappan's death saw continued, if generally smaller scale, sandalwood smuggling activity across the same border forests, carried out by numerous less individually notorious operators exploiting the same underlying pricing distortion that had sustained his career. Karnataka's state forest management policy, even after his death forced a period of public reckoning over the human cost of the state's sandalwood monopoly, continued for years afterward to exhibit many of the same structural features that had made illegal harvesting so persistently attractive, continuing to sell state harvested sandalwood to government processing factories at prices well below open market value, while maintaining harsh penalties, including significant fines and jail time, for private landowners whose own sandalwood trees were stolen or damaged, a policy combination that critics both within and outside the Indian conservation and legal community argued amounted to state maintained monopoly dressed in the language of conservation, protecting not the trees themselves so much as the state's own exclusive claim on the revenue they generated.

Veerappan's power over the two state governments hunting him became impossible to ignore after the night of July 30, 2000, when he and a band of roughly a dozen armed men attacked a farmhouse in Gajanur, in Tamil Nadu's Erode district, belonging to Dr. Rajkumar, the most revered actor in the history of Kannada cinema and a figure whose stature in Karnataka public life was difficult to overstate. Rajkumar had traveled to the property to conduct a housewarming ceremony. Veerappan's men arrived after dinner, entered the house, and told the family in Kannada that they had come for the actor. Rajkumar, his son in law, a relative, and an assistant film director were led out into the rain and marched into the forest. Before disappearing, Veerappan handed Rajkumar's wife a cassette tape with instructions that it be delivered directly to the Chief Minister of Karnataka.

The reaction inside Karnataka was immediate and volatile in its own right. Within hours of the news breaking, riots swept Bengaluru and other cities across the state. Offices belonging to four separate Tamil language newspapers were attacked by crowds who associated the abduction, however unfairly, with broader tensions between Karnataka and Tamil Nadu, tensions that had simmered for years over an unrelated dispute concerning shared river water from the Cauvery, the same river whose forested banks sheltered Veerappan's hideouts. The Kannada film industry shut down entirely in protest. Karnataka's chief minister, S. M. Krishna, traveled to Chennai within hours to meet his Tamil Nadu counterpart, M. Karunanidhi, and the two state governments, each nominally responsible for enforcing law within its own sandalwood forests, were forced into an uneasy joint crisis response to a hostage situation created by exactly the kind of forest bandit their own sandalwood monopoly policies had helped sustain for decades.

What followed was a hundred and eight day negotiation, conducted largely through a Tamil journalist named R. R. Gopal, editor of the magazine Nakkheeran, who was appointed by both state governments as chief intermediary and who conducted six separate rounds of talks with Veerappan's network over the following months. Veerappan's demands during this period extended well beyond simple ransom money into territory that exposed, with unusual clarity, just how much political leverage a sufficiently notorious forest bandit could accumulate against the machinery of two state governments. At one point during the crisis, Veerappan demanded that the long running Cauvery river water dispute between Karnataka and Tamil Nadu, a genuine and serious interstate conflict over water rights that predated him by decades and that neither state's own courts had been able to resolve, be referred to the International Court of Justice, a demand the two chief ministers were forced to publicly reject in a joint press conference even as they continued negotiating over the fate of the hostages. Rajkumar and his son in law were finally released on November 15, 2000, reportedly after a substantial ransom payment, though the precise terms of the eventual settlement were never fully disclosed by either government.

This was not, in fact, Veerappan's first experience using hostages as a tool of political negotiation with the state. In October 1997, in an episode that in retrospect served as a clear preview of the far higher stakes standoff to come, Veerappan kidnapped two wildlife photographers working near the Bandipur forest, then, the following day, seized fifteen tourists visiting the same area, including a government scientist. When Karnataka authorities dispatched six senior forest officials as part of the search and negotiation effort, Veerappan kidnapped them as well, absorbing the very state officials sent to rescue his earlier hostages into his growing collection of captives. Most of the tourists were released within twenty four hours, but Veerappan held onto several officials for close to seven weeks, using their captivity to press demands that included an official government pardon in exchange for their release, demands the state ultimately refused to grant even as it worked to secure the hostages' safety through prolonged negotiation.

The Rajkumar kidnapping proved to be the single event that most completely exposed the underlying dynamic this book is concerned with: a resource conflict rooted in an eighteenth century royal monopoly had, by the year 2000, grown powerful enough to force the elected chief ministers of two Indian states into humiliating public negotiation with a wanted killer, conducted through a private newspaper editor because neither government's own security apparatus, after years of dedicated Special Task Force operations, could locate Veerappan directly. India's Supreme Court later took a notably dim view of how both state governments had handled the crisis, criticizing what it characterized as capitulation to Veerappan's demands and raising pointed questions about the propriety of state authorities negotiating so extensively with an individual already wanted for the deaths of dozens of police officers and forest rangers. The episode remains, even now, a case study taught within Indian security and public administration circles precisely because it demonstrated so starkly how a resource monopoly born from an eighteenth century tax crisis could, two centuries later, briefly bring the machinery of two modern state governments to a standstill.

There is a particular kind of tragedy embedded in this outcome that deserves direct acknowledgment rather than glossing. The forests that Veerappan and his network devastated over three decades of illegal harvesting were, in ecological terms, genuinely irreplaceable within any human timescale relevant to the people actually living through this conflict. Santalum album requires thirty to sixty years to reach full commercial maturity. A tree cut down illegally in 1985, at relatively early stages of Veerappan's career, represented decades of accumulated biological growth destroyed in a single act, growth that no subsequent policy reform, however well designed, could restore within the lifetime of anyone alive at the time of the theft. The International Union for Conservation of Nature's 1997 classification of Santalum album as a vulnerable species was not an abstract bureaucratic designation. It reflected the cumulative, compounding damage of decades during which a state monopoly system created powerful financial incentives for exactly the kind of destructive, unsustainable harvesting that eventually threatened the long term survival of the species the monopoly claimed to be protecting.

Private cultivation of sandalwood was finally legalized within the broader Indian legal framework in 2001, three years before Veerappan's death, a reform that arrived, as with so much regulatory correction in resource management history, only after the crisis it addressed had already inflicted the bulk of its damage. Modern sandalwood plantations, established under this more liberalized legal regime, are today beginning to reach commercial maturity, offering a genuinely more sustainable path forward for the industry, one in which private landowners have direct financial incentive to protect and cultivate trees they are legally permitted to profit from, rather than being asked, as under the older system, to bear the risk of guarding a state owned asset for no personal financial benefit. But the thirty to sixty year maturation cycle that made sandalwood so valuable and so vulnerable to monopoly control in the first place means that the full effects of this 2001 reform will not be fully visible for decades yet to come, likely not until well past the middle of the twenty first century.

Veerappan's story, examined closely, offers a genuinely uncomfortable but historically important insight for anyone tempted to romanticize the scent trade wars this book documents as colorful historical curiosities safely confined to the past. The conditions that produced him, a state monopoly over a scarce, slow growing, extraordinarily valuable fragrant resource, priced by government fiat well below its true market value, enforced against impoverished local populations with limited alternative economic opportunities, are not a historical artifact belonging exclusively to the eighteenth or nineteenth centuries. They persisted, in substantially unmodified form, into the final years of the twentieth century and the opening years of the twenty first, and elements of that same underlying structural logic remain identifiable in Karnataka sandalwood policy even today. The particular man who exploited that gap with such sustained, lethal violence for over thirty years is gone, killed in an October forest ambush that Indian authorities were careful to photograph and publicize as definitive proof of the state's ultimate authority. But the economic architecture that made his three decade career possible in the first place, the same architecture Tipu Sultan first assembled in 1792 in the very different context of an eighteenth century kingdom bracing for renewed war with the British East India Company, has proven considerably more durable than any single bandit, however notorious, and considerably harder for any government to genuinely dismantle than to simply enforce, generation after generation, with steadily escalating force.

CHAPTER FOUR

Floating Gold

Of all the substances examined in this book, none has a stranger origin story than ambergris, and none has proven more stubbornly resistant to the ordinary tools governments use to control valuable commodities. For roughly a thousand years before its true biological source was definitively established, nobody trading in ambergris actually knew, with certainty, what it was. Merchants who moved it across the Islamic world, into China, and eventually into Renaissance Europe worked with a substance that arrived as a waxy, grey to black lump, faintly sweet and marine in scent when fresh, developing a complex, almost animalic, sweet fragrance as it aged, and that seemed to appear from nowhere, washed up on beaches with no discernible pattern, no visible source, and no method of cultivation. By the seventeenth century, no fewer than eighteen separate hypotheses had been proposed for its origin, variously attributing it to seals, crocodiles, sea birds, volcanic activity beneath the ocean floor, or simply an unusually dense and fragrant form of tree resin that had somehow ended up floating in the sea. Only once commercial whaling crews began systematically opening the carcasses of sperm whales in significant numbers did the actual answer become clear, and the answer, once discovered, was almost as strange as the mystery it replaced.

Ambergris, science eventually confirmed, forms inside the digestive tract of the sperm whale, apparently as a biological response to the sharp, indigestible beaks of the squid that make up a substantial part of the whale's diet. The beaks irritate the intestinal lining, and over time a waxy secretion, built around a compound called ambrein, forms around the accumulated hard material, eventually passing from the whale's body, most researchers now believe, primarily through vomiting rather than through the digestive tract's other end, though the exact mechanism has been debated across the scientific literature. Only a small fraction of sperm whales, current estimates suggest roughly one in a hundred, produce ambergris in commercially meaningful quantities at all, which means the substance was rare even at its biological source, before accounting for the additional improbability required for a piece to actually separate from a living or dead whale, survive the ocean environment, and eventually wash ashore somewhere a human being happened to be walking.

This combination of biological rarity and geographic randomness gives ambergris an economic character unlike almost any other commodity discussed in this book. Jasmine can be planted in a chosen field. Sandalwood, however slowly, can be cultivated on a chosen plot of land, at least once policy permits it. Ambergris cannot be farmed, cannot be reliably located through any known method beyond patient beachcombing and word of mouth networks, and cannot be produced on any predictable schedule whatsoever. It simply appears, or does not, on coastlines scattered across every ocean where sperm whales range, which is to say nearly the entire habitable planet, from the beaches of Sri Lanka and Mozambique to the coastlines of South Africa, Somalia, Yemen, and beyond. A find might be a small, unremarkable looking pebble worth a modest sum, or it might, in rare and celebrated cases, be a boulder sized mass worth well into six figures, discovered by an ordinary fisherman who had no idea, until he cut it open and caught the scent, that he was standing next to a genuine fortune.

The value that made ambergris worth pursuing across so many centuries and so many cultures rested on a specific and, for a long time, poorly understood chemical property. Ambergris functions as an extraordinarily effective fixative in perfumery, a substance that, added even in small quantities to a fragrance formula, dramatically slows the evaporation rate of more volatile scent components, allowing a perfume to retain its character and intensity on skin for far longer than the same formula would achieve without it. This property alone would have made ambergris commercially interesting, but its own distinctive scent, a complex, evolving combination of sweet, marine, and animalic notes that intensifies and mellows as the material ages, sometimes over decades, made it valuable in its own right as a fragrance component, not merely a technical additive. The finest, oldest, most weathered ambergris, cured by years of exposure to sun, salt water, and oxygen while floating or resting on a beach, commands prices that have historically rivaled, and in the contemporary market frequently exceed, the price of gold by weight.

The commercial history of ambergris predates any formal regulatory framework by centuries, which is precisely what makes its story so relevant to a book about scent trade conflicts. Throughout the sixteenth and seventeenth centuries, as European trading networks expanded into the Indian Ocean and beyond, ambergris moved through commercial channels with essentially no legal ownership framework governing who had the right to collect and sell it. Whoever found a piece on a beach could generally sell it, and disputes over ownership, when they arose, tended to be resolved through local custom rather than any codified maritime or property law. This absence of formal regulation created ample room for fraud alongside legitimate trade, and historical accounts from the period describe merchants substituting beeswax, tree resin, or shavings of aloe wood for genuine ambergris, exploiting buyers who had no reliable way to verify authenticity in an era before any scientific test for the substance existed. The line between ambergris trader and ambergris counterfeiter, in the earliest centuries of the trade, was often thinner than either party cared to admit.

The mystery surrounding ambergris's biological origin persisted stubbornly even as commercial whaling expanded dramatically through the eighteenth and nineteenth centuries, and it was really only through the industrial scale hunting of sperm whales, an enterprise pursued primarily for whale oil used in lighting and industrial lubrication rather than for ambergris itself, that whalers began routinely encountering ambergris directly inside the animals they killed, finally closing the scientific case on the substance's true origin. This is a genuinely uncomfortable historical fact worth stating plainly: the modern scientific understanding of ambergris arrived largely as an incidental byproduct of an entirely separate, massively destructive industrial hunting enterprise that would eventually push sperm whale populations to the brink of collapse across multiple ocean basins, an enterprise whose primary economic purpose had nothing to do with perfume at all.

The twentieth century brought the regulatory reckoning that ambergris's centuries of essentially unregulated trade had long postponed, though the reckoning arrived through a route that had little directly to do with ambergris itself. As global concern over collapsing whale populations intensified through the middle decades of the twentieth century, a wave of international and national protections emerged specifically targeting commercial whaling and the broader hunting of whale species, protections that, almost as a secondary consequence, swept ambergris into their scope even though ambergris itself, unlike whale oil or whale meat, does not require killing a whale to obtain. In the United States, the sperm whale was formally listed as an endangered species in 1970, and the subsequent Marine Mammal Protection Act and Endangered Species Act together established an outright prohibition on the possession or commercial trade of ambergris within American jurisdiction, a prohibition that remains in force today regardless of whether a given piece of ambergris was collected from a beach with no harm whatsoever to any living whale. Australia followed with its own comparable ban in 1999.

This regulatory approach created what might charitably be called an inconsistency, and what a less charitable observer might simply call a legal absurdity, at the heart of the modern ambergris trade, and it is an inconsistency that persists, largely unresolved, into the present day. The Convention on International Trade in Endangered Species, the primary international framework governing trade in products derived from protected animal species, explicitly distinguishes between products obtained by killing a protected animal and products, like naturally excreted ambergris, that a whale sheds without any human involvement whatsoever. Under CITES, naturally beached ambergris that has simply washed ashore is generally judged to fall outside the convention's core prohibitions, meaning it can be legally bought, sold, and exported in a substantial list of countries including the United Kingdom, Canada, France, Switzerland, and most Gulf Cooperation Council states, even though the same substance, if it happened to wash ashore on a beach in California or Queensland rather than Cornwall or Dubai, would expose its finder to serious criminal liability under domestic law in those jurisdictions.

The practical result of this patchwork, jurisdiction dependent legal landscape is a genuinely fragmented, deeply secretive global market that operates according to a logic almost unrecognizable from the transparent commodity exchanges that govern most other valuable natural materials. Ambergris dealers today typically maintain networks of informal, semi regular suppliers scattered across coastal communities with a documented history of significant finds, places like Sri Lanka, where fishermen frequently make the initial discovery, alongside Mozambique, South Africa, Somalia, and Yemen, and these dealers commonly travel enormous distances, sometimes across dozens of countries, chasing reports of a promising find, occasionally boarding a flight on short notice after hearing secondhand of a large discovery before a competitor can reach the same seller first. One prominent trader interviewed by journalists in recent years, a businessman based in the United Arab Emirates who deals primarily in silver and gold but treats ambergris as a lucrative and personally enjoyable sideline, described placing advertisements in local newspapers while traveling specifically to solicit ambergris suppliers, a marketing method that would seem almost quaint if the underlying product were not routinely valued in the hundreds of thousands of dollars per transaction.

For traders operating from jurisdictions where the substance remains outright illegal, secrecy is not simply a business preference but a genuine legal necessity, and this has pushed a meaningful share of the global ambergris trade into channels that function, in practice, indistinguishably from other forms of black market wildlife trafficking, even though the underlying material itself involves no direct harm to any living animal. Indian authorities, who classify ambergris as property of the central government under domestic law regardless of CITES's more permissive international framework, have conducted repeated, well publicized raids against ambergris smuggling networks in recent years. A single sting operation in Tamil Nadu netted two suspected smugglers along with eight kilograms of ambergris valued at approximately one million dollars, part of a broader pattern that saw six separate seizures across Mumbai and Thane in a single summer, seizures that Indian authorities have explicitly connected to organized criminal networks operating a genuinely international trafficking pipeline that treats ambergris with the same operational seriousness typically associated with narcotics or trafficked ivory.

The scale of the contemporary legitimate ambergris market, insofar as it can be estimated given the substance's inherent secrecy, has grown considerably in recent years, driven substantially by a broader consumer shift toward premium natural ingredients with genuine, verifiable provenance stories across the luxury personal care and fragrance industries. Industry analysis places European ambergris market revenue alone at roughly one hundred and ninety eight million dollars in a recent year, representing close to a third of the estimated global total, a dominance the European market owes largely to its historical position as the trade's central hub for luxury perfumery combined with the relatively permissive regulatory environment several key European jurisdictions maintain toward naturally sourced material under the CITES framework. Current industry estimates suggest that somewhere between sixty and sixty five percent of global commercial ambergris transactions occur within jurisdictions where the trade remains fully legal, with the remainder split between outright grey market channels and a smaller category of transactions conducted under specific, tightly controlled regulatory permissions granted for pharmaceutical research purposes.

The persistence of scientific interest in ambergris despite the emergence of synthetic fixative alternatives is itself worth noting, because it illustrates a pattern that recurs throughout the history of natural scent materials: synthetic replacements, however chemically sophisticated, have rarely managed to fully displace demand for the genuine natural article among the highest end luxury perfume houses, who continue to market natural ambergris sourcing as a point of authenticity and prestige distinguishing their most expensive formulations from mass market competitors relying entirely on laboratory synthesized substitutes. Houses including Chanel and Lanvin have historically prized genuine ambergris specifically for this combination of technical fixative performance and irreplaceable scent complexity, qualities that decades of advancing synthetic chemistry have approximated with growing sophistication but never, according to the most demanding perfumers, fully replicated.

What makes ambergris's story genuinely distinctive within the broader pattern this book traces is the near total absence of any single government, dynasty, or colonial authority ever having successfully asserted meaningful territorial control over its supply, in the manner Tipu Sultan achieved, however imperfectly, over Mysore's sandalwood forests, or that Grasse's perfume houses achieved over the flower fields of Provence. Ambergris simply cannot be controlled through the traditional mechanisms of land ownership, royal decree, or agricultural monopoly that have governed nearly every other scent trade examined in these pages, precisely because it originates inside a wide ranging ocean mammal and arrives on shore at essentially random points along thousands of miles of coastline, obeying no administrative boundary and respecting no claimed royal forest. India's assertion of central government ownership over any ambergris found within its territory represents perhaps the most serious modern attempt at exactly this kind of territorial control, and even that assertion, as the recurring pattern of seizures and prosecutions makes clear, has proven only partially effective against a trade that a finder can, with sufficient discretion, simply carry across a border and sell somewhere the material is perfectly legal.

This is, in its own quiet way, a genuinely important variation on the broader theme running through this book. Every other scent trade war examined here, the sandalwood forests of Mysore, the flower fields of Grasse, the rose valleys of Bulgaria explored in the chapter that follows, the frankincense coast of Somaliland, ultimately concerns a fixed, geographically locatable resource that a sufficiently determined authority can, at least in principle, fence off, tax, and defend. Ambergris resists this logic entirely. It belongs to no one until someone happens to find it, it can wash ashore anywhere a sperm whale has ever swum, which is to say nearly everywhere, and no ruler, however powerful, has ever managed to declare an ocean current a royal possession in any way that could actually be enforced. In this sense, ambergris represents something close to the purest possible test case for whether scarcity and desire alone, absent any government's ability to physically control the source, are sufficient to sustain a genuine, centuries spanning global trade network. The answer, four hundred years of evidence overwhelmingly suggests, is yes.

CHAPTER FIVE

The Valley That Bled Perfume

Between two mountain ranges in central Bulgaria, the Balkan range to the north and the Sredna Gora to the south, lies a long, narrow valley that has produced, for more than three centuries, some of the most prized rose oil in the entire history of perfumery. The valley takes its popular name directly from the crop that made it famous, the Rose Valley, and its two principal towns, Kazanlak and Karlovo, remain today the historic and commercial heart of an industry whose product, known variously as attar of roses or rose otto, has for generations commanded prices among the highest of any natural essential oil produced anywhere on earth. To understand why this particular valley, and not any of the countless other places in the world where roses grow, became the epicenter of an industry powerful enough to shape provincial Ottoman administration, one has to start with the flower itself, and with the peculiar combination of climate, soil, and human labor that made this specific stretch of Balkan countryside so improbably well suited to producing it.

The rose responsible for Bulgaria's fame is not, despite the valley's popular name, native to the region at all. Rosa damascena, the damask rose, most likely arrived in the Bulgarian lands from the Middle East sometime after the Ottoman conquest of the Balkans, carried, according to regional tradition, by Ottoman traders or officials sometime around the turn of the eighteenth century, with documented evidence placing organized cultivation in the Karlovo region as early as 1712. What the rose found upon arrival was a set of growing conditions that, almost by accident, turned out to be even more favorable than those in its original Middle Eastern homeland. The valley's specific combination of mild winters, moderate rainfall during the crucial May and June flowering period, and distinctive cinnamon colored forest soils created conditions that Bulgarian rose growers themselves, along with generations of visiting perfumers, would come to describe as measurably superior to the growing conditions the same rose species experienced in Tunisia, Syria, or Turkey, producing a flower with a notably higher oil content and a more complex, longer lasting fragrance profile than damask roses grown almost anywhere else on earth.

By the nineteenth century, the towns of Kazanlak and Karlovo had become established centers of an industrial scale rose oil production operation supplying markets across Europe and, increasingly, well beyond it. The traditional production method, refined over generations of Bulgarian practice, involved a distillation apparatus known locally as a gyulpana, essentially a cauldron and lid arrangement adapted from techniques Bulgarian producers had already mastered through centuries of brandy distillation in the same region, a technical inheritance that turned out to translate remarkably well to the very different challenge of extracting delicate floral oils without degrading their fragrance through excessive heat. Bulgarian producers developed a double distillation process that increased extraction yields substantially compared to the single distillation methods more commonly used elsewhere, a genuine technical innovation that gave Bulgarian rose oil both a quantitative production advantage and a qualitative reputation advantage that together cemented the valley's position as the preeminent rose oil producing region in the world.

The scale of this production by the mid nineteenth century was genuinely industrial in character, even though the underlying labor remained almost entirely manual and seasonal. Historical records from the Kazanlak region document that by 1860, the area was operating some 1,271 individual distillation cauldrons across its various producing villages, with individual settlements like Aleksandrovo and Shipka each running well over a hundred cauldrons of their own, a concentration of processing capacity that reflected just how central rose cultivation and distillation had become to the entire regional economy by that point. Each cauldron, over the course of a single rose harvesting season, could produce roughly one hundred and thirty five vials of rose water and its associated oil, a production rhythm dictated entirely by the extraordinarily narrow harvest window during which the roses could be picked, a window that opened and closed within a matter of weeks each May and June, exactly as with the jasmine and rose harvests of Grasse examined earlier in this book, and imposing the same brutal, unforgiving seasonal logic on every family and workshop involved in the trade.

This narrow harvest window, combined with the sheer economic significance rose oil had come to hold for the region by the middle of the nineteenth century, meant that the towns of the Rose Valley existed under conditions of near total economic dependency on a single, highly seasonal, weather sensitive crop, precisely the kind of concentrated economic vulnerability that, throughout this book, has repeatedly proven capable of transforming ordinary agricultural administration into genuine political conflict. And the Rose Valley did not exist in a political vacuum. It sat, throughout the entire period of its rise to international prominence, within the Ottoman Empire, under an imperial administrative system that by the middle of the nineteenth century was under severe and mounting financial strain, a strain that inevitably found its way, through one channel or another, into the tax burdens imposed on productive agricultural regions across the empire's Balkan territories.

The specific administrative structure governing Ottoman Bulgaria through much of this period relied heavily on a decentralized system in which local Muslim officials and tax farmers, individuals granted the right to collect taxes on behalf of the imperial treasury in exchange for a share of the proceeds, exercised substantial practical authority over how agricultural revenue was actually extracted from producing regions like the Rose Valley. This tax farming system, common across large stretches of the Ottoman Empire, created strong incentives for local tax farmers to extract as much revenue as possible from productive local industries, since their own personal income depended directly on the margin between what they collected from producers and what they were contractually obligated to remit to Constantinople. A high value, internationally traded commodity like rose oil, with its established European export markets and correspondingly higher achievable prices, represented an especially attractive target for this kind of intensive local tax extraction, precisely because rose oil producers, unlike subsistence farmers growing grain primarily for local consumption, had genuine hard currency income from export sales that a tax farmer could realistically claim a share of.

The broader financial crisis gripping the Ottoman state through the middle of the 1870s made this dynamic considerably worse. Facing the serious prospect of state bankruptcy, the imperial government moved in 1875 to raise taxes significantly across its territories, with the burden falling with particular severity on non Muslim populations within the empire, a category that included the substantial majority of the population across Ottoman Bulgaria, including the rose growing communities of Kazanlak and Karlovo. This tax increase landed on a Balkan population already straining under decades of accumulated grievances regarding Ottoman administration, grievances that extended well beyond simple taxation to encompass questions of legal status, political representation, and basic civil treatment under an imperial system that formally privileged its Muslim subjects over its Christian ones in numerous respects.

It would be historically inaccurate, and this book has no interest in overstating its case, to claim that rose oil taxation was the primary or even a major direct cause of the broader Bulgarian national uprising that erupted in the spring of 1876, an uprising whose deeper roots lay in a complex, decades long buildup of nationalist sentiment, religious tension, and genuine political grievance that extended across the entire Ottoman Balkan territory and encompassed populations who had nothing whatsoever to do with the rose trade. But it is entirely accurate, and historically well documented, to note that the same increased tax burden driving broader unrest across Ottoman Bulgaria in 1875 fell directly and heavily on the rose producing communities of the Sub Balkan valley, a region whose local prosperity, unusual by the standards of the broader Balkan peasant economy of the period, depended almost entirely on continued profitable access to European rose oil export markets, access that heavier local taxation, whatever its ultimate destination in

Constantinople's strained treasury, directly threatened to undermine.

The uprising that broke out across Ottoman Bulgaria in April 1876, organized by a network of revolutionary committees and intended as a coordinated, empire wide rebellion, instead erupted prematurely in several districts after Ottoman authorities uncovered elements of the plot, triggering a brutal and disproportionate response from irregular Ottoman militia forces known as bashi bazouks. The suppression that followed produced what contemporary British and American journalists, most notably the correspondent Januarius MacGahan, would describe to a horrified European public as the Bulgarian Horrors, a campaign of village burnings and civilian massacres that claimed, by the most credible contemporary estimates, somewhere between twelve thousand and thirty thousand Bulgarian lives, concentrated with particular horror in towns including Batak, where irregular forces killed thousands of civilians despite an initially negotiated surrender. The international outcry these reports generated across Europe, particularly within Britain, where public opinion turned sharply and unexpectedly against an Ottoman government London had traditionally treated as a strategic ally, proved decisive in shifting European diplomatic support toward Bulgarian national aspirations, ultimately contributing to the re establishment of an independent Bulgarian state following the Russo Turkish War of 1877 and 1878.

The Rose Valley itself, positioned squarely within the geographic heart of Ottoman Bulgaria, did not escape this broader convulsion, and its rose growing communities, whatever the precise degree to which rose taxation specifically motivated local participation in the uprising and its suppression, experienced the same catastrophic disruption that swept across the wider Bulgarian countryside during 1876 and the war years that followed. Fields went untended during a period when armies, irregular militias, and eventually the advancing Russian imperial forces that would liberate Bulgaria moved repeatedly through the same territory that had, only a few years earlier, been quietly producing the world's most valuable rose oil for export to the perfume houses of Paris and London. It is a measure of the underlying strength and resilience of the region's rose growing tradition, refined over more than a century and a half of accumulated technical expertise by 1876, that the industry recovered relatively quickly once an independent Bulgarian state was established, resuming and eventually expanding production through the final decades of the nineteenth century and into the twentieth.

The new Bulgarian state that emerged from the crisis of the 1870s, unlike the Ottoman administration it replaced, had genuine domestic political incentive to actively support and promote an industry that represented one of the country's few internationally competitive, hard currency earning export sectors, and rose oil cultivation expanded significantly under Bulgarian national administration through the following decades. By 1917, at what would prove to be the historical peak of Bulgarian rose cultivation, the industry's planted area reached nearly nine thousand hectares spread across the Sub Balkan valley system, an expansion that reflected both growing international demand and a level of state supported agricultural investment that would have been considerably harder to achieve under the more extractive, less locally accountable administrative structure of the late Ottoman period.

The industry's twentieth century history was not without further severe disruption, most significantly during the transition from a state directed socialist economy under Bulgaria's communist government to a market driven system following the political changes of the early 1990s, a transition that forced substantial and often painful structural adjustment across the entire Bulgarian rose oil sector as decades old state production and distribution arrangements were dismantled and replaced with more fragmented private enterprise. Despite this disruption, the underlying industry survived and, in the decades since, has successfully rebuilt its position as one of the most significant rose oil producing regions remaining anywhere in the world, still concentrated in the same five core producing areas of Kazanlak, Karlovo, Streltcha, Zelinkovo, and Chirpan that have anchored the trade for well over a century.

Contemporary Bulgaria today accounts for a substantial share of total global rose oil production, competing primarily against Turkey as the world's other major producer of genuine damask rose oil, with the two countries together supplying the overwhelming majority of natural rose oil used across the international perfume and cosmetics industry. Kazanlak itself has, in the decades since Bulgaria's transition away from centralized socialist economic planning, developed a substantial tourism industry built directly around its rose heritage, anchored by an annual Rose Festival held each June at the peak of the flowering season, during which visitors from across Europe and increasingly from further afield travel to the valley specifically to witness traditional hand harvesting demonstrations, tour working distilleries still using methods recognizably descended from the eighteenth century gyulpana apparatus described earlier in this chapter, and purchase rose oil and rose water products directly from the producing region, a heritage tourism model that echoes, in its broad structure, the UNESCO recognition and cultural heritage branding strategy this book's later chapters will show Grasse itself pursuing as its own raw agricultural acreage contracted through the second half of the twentieth century.

What the Bulgarian rose story adds to this book's broader argument is a genuinely important variation on the themes already established in Grasse and in Mysore. Unlike Grasse, where local perfume houses accumulated influence over provincial French administrators through sustained economic leverage exercised within a relatively stable, functioning state, and unlike Mysore, where a single ruler's deliberate monopoly decision shaped two centuries of subsequent conflict, Bulgaria's rose trade found itself, largely as an accident of geography and imperial administrative structure, caught within the machinery of a far larger and more violent political crisis, one whose fundamental causes extended well beyond any single agricultural commodity but whose local economic texture, the specific tax burdens imposed on specific producing communities, the specific export income those communities stood to lose, was nonetheless shaped in real and documented ways by the presence of an internationally valuable, highly taxable export crop growing in their fields. The rose growers of Kazanlak and Karlovo did not choose the uprising that swept through their valley in 1876, and they did not cause it. But they lived, worked, and in some cases died within a regional economy whose particular value, the fragrant oil that made their valley famous across Europe, had made their communities a specific, identifiable target for exactly the kind of intensified late Ottoman tax extraction that helped drive so many of their Balkan neighbors, across trades that had nothing to do with roses at all, to the same breaking point in the same terrible spring.

CHAPTER SIX

The Deer That Could Not Be Farmed

High in the alpine and subalpine forests of the Himalaya, above the treeline where rhododendron and dwarf bamboo give way to lichen covered rock, lives one of the shyest and most consistently misunderstood animals ever to enter the history of perfumery. The musk deer is a small, solitary creature, standing under a meter at the shoulder, entirely without antlers, and distinguished instead by long, downward curving canine tusks in the males that give the animal a faintly prehistoric appearance utterly unlike the familiar spotted deer of lowland forests. It survives on a sparse alpine diet of lichens, mosses, and low shrubs at elevations between three and four and a half thousand meters, is almost entirely nocturnal in its habits, and would, under any reasonable set of circumstances, have remained one of the most obscure mammals in the Himalayan ecosystem, known only to the handful of specialists who study high altitude wildlife. Instead, it became the target of one of the most sustained and economically consequential poaching campaigns in the entire history of the global fragrance trade, hunted relentlessly across a mountain range spanning half a dozen countries for a single, tiny gland that a male deer carries beneath its abdomen.

That gland, known as the musk pod, produces a waxy secretion that male musk deer use to mark territory and attract mates during the breeding season, and it is this secretion, dried and processed, that gives natural musk its name and its extraordinary, centuries spanning value in perfumery. Musk possesses a deep, warm, animalic scent that functions, much like ambergris discussed in an earlier chapter, as an exceptionally effective fixative, extending the life of more volatile fragrance components while contributing its own distinctive, difficult to replicate character to a finished perfume. For most of recorded history, prior to the development of synthetic musk compounds in the twentieth century, natural deer musk was essentially irreplaceable in fine perfumery, a single ingredient with no meaningful substitute, which meant that demand for it, across markets stretching from traditional Chinese medicine to European luxury fragrance houses, remained persistently, and in commercial terms almost uniquely, inelastic.

Musk's documented trading history stretches back considerably further than most of the other conflicts examined in this book, reaching at least into the early centuries of the common era, when the substance traveled westward from Central Asia and Tibet along the network of overland caravan routes historians would eventually name the Silk Road, carried alongside silk, spices, and other high value, low bulk luxury goods well suited to the slow, expensive logistics of overland caravan transport across some of the most forbidding terrain on the Eurasian landmass. Musk's specific value within this broader luxury trade rested on precisely the combination of qualities that would sustain demand for it across the following fifteen centuries: an extraordinarily high value relative to its weight and volume, a genuine irreplaceability within the perfumery and medicinal traditions of virtually every major civilization along the trade route, from Tang dynasty China through the Islamic caliphates of the Middle East to the royal courts of medieval Europe, and a source confined to a genuinely remote, difficult to access mountain region that few outside the immediate area could realistically hope to control directly. Arab traders operating across this network are recorded as having developed their own specific grading and quality assessment terminology for musk of different regional origins, distinguishing Tibetan musk from varieties sourced further east, a level of specialized commercial sophistication that illustrates just how significant and well established the trade had already become well over a thousand years before the first CITES protections were ever contemplated.

The economics of musk extraction are what transformed this obscure alpine animal into a genuine international commodity crisis. A single mature male musk deer produces only twenty five to thirty grams of musk in its pod, an almost absurdly small yield relative to the animal's overall size and the effort required to locate and kill it in genuinely remote, difficult high altitude terrain. Unlike sandalwood, which at least offers the theoretical possibility of harvesting oil from a tree without destroying it entirely, or ambergris, which requires no killing whatsoever, traditional musk extraction has historically been an unambiguously lethal process: the pod is removed after the animal is killed, meaning every gram of musk that entered the historical trade represented, in the overwhelming majority of cases, one dead deer, regardless of whether the pod's contents ultimately proved to be of high or disappointingly low quality once processed.

This brutal extraction ratio, an entire animal's life traded for a few grams of glandular secretion, combined with musk's persistent irreplaceability in perfumery for most of human history, to create a market dynamic of genuinely extreme price intensity. On the black market that has dominated the musk trade since international protections tightened through the second half of the twentieth century, musk routinely fetches prices reaching into the thousands of dollars per kilogram, a valuation that, translated into per animal terms given each deer's tiny individual yield, meant that even a single successful hunt could represent a meaningful cash windfall for hunters operating in some of the poorest, most economically marginal rural communities anywhere in Asia, communities scattered across the high altitude borderlands of Nepal, India, Bhutan, China, Mongolia, and the broader Central Asian range where the various musk deer species are found.

The geographic range of musk deer populations, extending in a broad arc from the Russian Far East and the Korean peninsula, around the Gobi desert into China, through the entire Himalayan region, and into Afghanistan and Pakistan, meant that the trade in musk was never a single, geographically containable industry in the way the sandalwood trade was substantially confined to southern India, or the rose trade to a single Bulgarian valley. It was instead a genuinely transnational hunting and smuggling economy that crossed some of the most politically sensitive, poorly governed, and historically contested borders anywhere in Asia, borders separating countries with vastly different levels of enforcement capacity, wildly divergent domestic legal frameworks, and, in several cases, deeply strained bilateral political relationships that made any kind of coordinated cross border conservation enforcement extraordinarily difficult to organize and sustain.

International recognition of the crisis facing musk deer populations arrived relatively early compared to some of the other conflicts examined in this book. The species was brought under the protection of the Convention on International Trade in Endangered Species in 1979, with populations across Afghanistan, Bhutan, India, Myanmar, Nepal, and Pakistan placed under the Convention's most restrictive category, Appendix I, a designation that prohibits international commercial trade entirely in wild sourced specimens or their parts. Musk deer populations in other parts of their range received the somewhat less restrictive Appendix II designation, permitting trade under strict monitoring and permit requirements rather than an outright ban, a split listing structure that reflected the genuinely fragmented, population specific conservation status of a species whose numbers varied enormously across its vast geographic range, from the comparatively healthier populations estimated in Russia's Far East, at roughly one hundred and forty thousand animals in recent surveys, to the severely depleted, difficult to accurately count populations scattered across the more heavily hunted and habitat pressured stretches of the Himalayan range itself.

This 1979 CITES listing, whatever its genuine conservation intentions, produced exactly the pattern that this book has now documented across sandalwood, ambergris, and, to a lesser degree, Bulgarian rose oil: a formal legal prohibition that, rather than eliminating demand, simply pushed an already lucrative trade further underground, raising black market prices even higher by restricting legal supply while doing comparatively little to address the underlying economic desperation that made musk hunting so attractive to impoverished mountain communities in the first place. Decades after the 1979 listing, illegal musk deer poaching remains a persistent, well documented problem across the species's Himalayan range, driven overwhelmingly by continued demand from the international perfume industry alongside sustained demand from traditional Chinese and other Asian medicine systems that have used musk as a component in various remedies for centuries, entirely independent of and predating its use in Western perfumery.

The Nepal China border, running along some of the most remote and historically porous stretches of the entire Himalayan frontier, has emerged repeatedly in wildlife trafficking investigations as a particularly active corridor for musk and other high value wildlife product smuggling, a pattern documented in detail through the crossing point at Urai in Nepal's Bajhang district, where local reporting has traced a persistent, multi decade pattern of illegal cross border trade in medicinal herbs and wildlife parts, including musk deer products alongside tiger bone and pelt, moving from Nepal into Tibet and onward into broader Chinese markets. The specific administrative history of this crossing point illustrates, in miniature, exactly the kind of governance vacuum that has allowed musk trafficking to persist for so long despite decades of formal international protection. A temporary Nepal Police security post that had operated seasonally at this crossing was displaced during the period of Maoist insurgency that gripped rural Nepal beginning around 2000, and although a nearby border police post was eventually reinstated following the 2006 peace agreement that formally ended the insurgency, the original Kalanga area post itself was never fully reestablished, leaving a documented, persistent gap in border enforcement capacity precisely along one of the routes most actively used by wildlife and medicinal herb smugglers moving product toward Chinese buyers.

The Covid nineteen pandemic, and the accompanying nationwide lockdowns and border closures that followed across South Asia beginning in early 2020, might reasonably have been expected to disrupt this kind of cross border smuggling activity, given the severe general restrictions placed on movement and trade across the entire region during this period. Local reporting from Bajhang district instead documented the opposite pattern: even as the Chinese government formally sealed its side of the border in January 2020 specifically in response to pandemic concerns, illegal cross border trade in medicinal herbs and wildlife parts, coordinated between local Nepali traders and Chinese counterparts operating from the Tibetan town of Taklakot, continued and by some local accounts actually intensified through the months that followed, as the same collapse in ordinary legal economic activity that devastated legitimate cross border commerce appears to have pushed some local communities toward greater reliance on the illegal trade as one of the few income sources still functioning across a border that legitimate goods could no longer easily cross.

Conservation efforts targeting musk deer populations have taken several distinct forms across the range countries most affected by the trade, reflecting genuinely different national approaches to the same underlying species conservation challenge. India has pursued a strategy centered on captive breeding, most prominently through the Kanchula Kharak Musk Deer Breeding Centre in the northern state of Uttarakhand, established with the explicit goal of producing musk through a sustainable captive extraction process that does not require killing the animal, an approach that, if successfully scaled, could in principle satisfy at least a portion of ongoing international demand without further depleting wild populations. Musk deer farms pursuing broadly similar captive breeding and non lethal extraction models have also been established in China and, on a smaller scale, in Nepal, and there is documented evidence, including successful musk extraction conducted repeatedly over several years at facilities including Nepal's own Kathmandu zoo, that non lethal extraction from living, captive animals is technically achievable, offering a genuine, if still limited, alternative to the traditional lethal harvest model that has driven the species toward its current conservation crisis.

Whether captive breeding and farming can realistically substitute for wild sourced musk at anything approaching the scale needed to eliminate the underlying black market incentive remains, even now, a genuinely open and actively debated question within the conservation and wildlife trade policy community. Musk deer are notoriously difficult animals to breed and maintain successfully in captivity, exhibiting high stress sensitivity and correspondingly poor breeding success rates in many captive settings, limitations that have so far prevented captive musk production from scaling to anything close to the volume that would be needed to meaningfully undercut black market prices for wild sourced product. In the meantime, the fundamental economic calculation that has sustained musk poaching for well over a century remains, in most of the species's Himalayan range, essentially unchanged: a desperately poor rural hunter, operating in one of the most economically marginal regions on the entire planet, can still realistically expect to earn more from a single successful musk deer kill than from months of alternative available labor, an equation that no amount of formal CITES protection has yet managed to fully rewrite.

The species's current conservation status reflects the cumulative weight of this century long pressure with sobering clarity. The Himalayan musk deer carries an Endangered classification on the International Union for Conservation of Nature's Red List, with a population trend that continues to be assessed as declining across most of its range despite more than four decades of nominal international legal protection under CITES. In India specifically, the species receives the highest possible domestic legal protection available under the Wildlife Protection Act of 1972, a Schedule I classification that places it in the same protective category as the country's most iconic and closely guarded endangered species, a legal status that has nonetheless proven insufficient, on its own, to halt continued poaching pressure across the species's Uttarakhand, Himachal Pradesh, Sikkim, and Arunachal Pradesh range within Indian territory.

What the musk deer trade adds to this book's broader argument, distinct from the lessons of sandalwood, ambergris, and Bulgarian rose oil already examined, is a particularly stark illustration of how a scent trade conflict can persist and even intensify across some of the most heavily governed, internationally scrutinized borders in the world, borders separating nuclear armed states with sophisticated formal security apparatus, and still remain functionally unenforceable at the level of individual mountain crossings where formal state presence has proven, across decades of documented experience, thin, inconsistent, and repeatedly vulnerable to displacement by broader political crises entirely unrelated to wildlife trafficking itself. Sandalwood could at least, in principle, be fenced and patrolled within a single country's forest department jurisdiction. Musk deer range across the sovereign territory of half a dozen nations, each with its own laws, its own enforcement priorities, and its own capacity constraints, and the animal itself, solitary, nocturnal, and adapted to some of the most inaccessible terrain on the planet, has proven exceptionally difficult to protect through any strategy that has not, so far, managed to close the fundamental economic gap between what a musk pod is worth on the black market and what a subsistence hunter in the high Himalaya has any realistic alternative way of earning.

CHAPTER SEVEN

Frankincense Coast

No scent trade examined in this book stretches back further into recorded human history than the resin trade of the northern Somali coast, a commerce so ancient that it appears in the earliest surviving Egyptian trade records, so consequential that Roman naturalists devoted entire sections of their encyclopedic works to it, and so persistently misattributed across two thousand years of Western commentary that its actual geographic origin was, for most of that history, systematically obscured rather than illuminated by the very civilizations that depended on it most. The story of frankincense and myrrh is, among all the conflicts this book examines, the one with the deepest roots and, in certain respects, the most quietly enduring modern relevance, connecting the mist forests of the Golis Mountains directly to contemporary Christian liturgy, Arabian household custom, Chinese traditional medicine, and the perfume counters of Paris, all sourced from the same stubborn, spiky trees that have grown on the same mountain slopes for millennia.

Frankincense and myrrh are both aromatic gum resins, harvested through an identical basic method that has changed remarkably little across thousands of years of continuous practice. Harvesters make deliberate incisions in the bark of the producing trees, and the wounded tree responds by exuding a milky sap that hardens on contact with air into the small, irregular, stone like nuggets of resin that constitute the actual traded commodity. Frankincense comes specifically from Boswellia trees, which in the Somali context grow at the higher elevations of the Golis range, while myrrh derives from Commiphora myrrha, which favors the somewhat lower, drier slopes below the frankincense zone. Two distinct Boswellia species have particular significance to the Somali trade specifically: Boswellia sacra, known locally as moxor, which produces a resin called beeyo, and Boswellia frereana, called yagcar locally, which produces a resin known as meydi and which has the added distinction of being found, as a distinct endemic species, nowhere else on earth outside the Somali frankincense growing region.

The economic and cultural significance of this trade to the ancient world is difficult to overstate, and it long predates any conventional dating of organized commerce in most other regions examined in this book. Ancient Egyptian trade expeditions to a region the Egyptians recorded as the Land of Punt, which most Egyptologists today place somewhere within the modern Horn of Africa, sought myrrh, frankincense, and related resinous gums as central objectives of their voyages, establishing a documented trading relationship that predates the classical Greek and Roman periods by well over a thousand years. By the time Rome had risen to dominate Mediterranean commerce, the natural historian Pliny the Elder devoted substantial attention to frankincense within his sprawling encyclopedic work Natural History, treating the substance as one of the genuinely significant commodities of the ancient world, worthy of extended scholarly discussion alongside gold, precious stones, and the other treasures that most preoccupied Roman commercial and intellectual attention.

And it is here that the deepest and most persistent injustice in the entire history of the frankincense trade becomes visible. Pliny himself, reflecting the broader consensus understanding of his era, wrote confidently that Arabia alone produced frankincense, and that myrrh, while also found in Arabia, was shared only with what Roman writers called the Cave Dwellers Country, a designation that entirely excluded the actual African coast where a substantial share, quite possibly the majority, of the ancient world's frankincense and myrrh genuinely originated. This was not simply an innocent geographic error born of limited ancient knowledge. Contemporary historians studying the trade have identified this systematic Arabian attribution as reflecting, at least in part, the deliberate secrecy that Arabian intermediary traders maintained regarding the true African source of much of the resin passing through their hands, a commercial strategy that protected their own position as essential middlemen controlling access to a valuable commodity whose actual origin, if widely known, might have allowed Mediterranean buyers to bypass Arabian intermediaries and trade directly with African producers instead. Compounding this deliberate obscuring, the broader racial and cultural biases prevalent among ancient Mediterranean writers toward African societies made it, in the assessment of modern historians examining this period, considerably easier for a systematically incomplete and Arabia centered account of the trade's true geography to take hold and persist across the classical written record for centuries, obscuring the genuine African origin of goods that had, in reality, moved through Somali coastal ports for as long as organized long distance trade in the region had existed at all.

The port towns that anchored this trade along the northern Somali coastline developed into genuinely significant commercial centers in their own right across the classical and medieval periods, competing directly with major established trading powers of the ancient Indo Greco Roman commercial world including the Sabaean kingdom of southern Arabia, the Parthian empire, and the Aksumite kingdom centered in the Ethiopian highlands, all of whom sought access to the same lucrative resin trade routes running through the Horn of Africa and across the Red Sea and Indian Ocean toward Mediterranean and South Asian markets. Berbera, in particular, emerged as the dominant marketplace along the entire Somali seaboard, a position it would maintain, with periodic interruption, across an extraordinary span of continuous commercial history. By the early nineteenth century, contemporary accounts describe Berbera's annual trading season swelling the town's population to over seventy thousand people at its seasonal peak, with as many as six thousand camels arriving laden with interior goods within a single day during the height of trading activity, figures that illustrate just how significant this single Somali port had become as a commercial hub for an enormous range of goods moving between the African interior and international maritime trade networks, of which frankincense and myrrh remained among the most consistently valuable and internationally sought after.

The colonial period brought new administrative structures to this ancient trading system, structures that, as in so many of the conflicts examined throughout this book, sought to impose formal territorial and political control over a commerce that had for millennia operated according to its own established, largely self regulating patterns of production, transport, and exchange. British Somaliland existed as a formal colonial protectorate from the late nineteenth century until 1960, governed across this period by a succession of colonial governors whose administrative authority extended, at least in principle, over the frankincense and myrrh producing regions of the Golis Mountains and the trading infrastructure of ports including Berbera. The formal historical record of these colonial administrations, meticulously documented in surviving British colonial archives listing each successive governor's tenure across the decades of protectorate rule, reflects the broader pattern this book has traced repeatedly: territories whose genuine underlying economic significance rested substantially on an ancient, geographically specific resource trade, now folded into modern administrative and political structures whose colonial officials had to reckon, whether they fully understood it or not, with commercial patterns and trading relationships that predated their own arrival by thousands of years.

Somalia's post independence political history brought a further, and in important respects more directly damaging, chapter to the frankincense and myrrh trade's long history, this time under the specific policies of the military government led by Mohamed Siad Barre, which governed Somalia from 1969 until its collapse in the early 1990s. Under Barre's administration, the frankincense and myrrh sector was formally nationalized under a state entity known as the Frankincense and Gums Trading Agency, an arrangement that placed the ancient trade, for the first time in its multi thousand year history, under direct, centralized state control and management. Rather than modernizing or professionalizing the industry, this nationalization is widely documented, in subsequent historical and journalistic accounts of the period, as having instead folded the frankincense trade into the broader pattern of corruption and dysfunctional state bureaucracy that characterized the Barre government's economic management more generally, a period that saw the trade's genuine commercial vitality substantially diminished under the weight of centralized mismanagement, precisely the opposite outcome that state control efforts examined elsewhere in this book, from Mysore's sandalwood monopoly to Bulgaria's later state directed rose oil industry, might have led one to expect from formal government involvement in a valuable natural resource sector.

The collapse of the Barre government in 1991, and the subsequent declaration of independence by the northern territory of Somaliland, a declaration that remains, even now, unrecognized by the broader international community despite Somaliland's decades long record of functioning largely independently from the ongoing conflict and instability that has continued to affect southern Somalia, opened a new and in significant respects more positive chapter for the frankincense and myrrh trade. Freed from the specific bureaucratic and corrupt state control structures that had constrained the industry under Barre's centralized nationalization policy, gum and resin production and trade in Somaliland began a gradual but sustained recovery through the 1990s and into the following decades, resuming its historical role as one of the territory's most economically significant export sectors, trailing only livestock in overall importance to the Somaliland economy.

Contemporary accounts of the trade document its continued, substantial economic significance to rural communities across northern Somalia even today, with one industry estimate placing exports at roughly three hundred and thirty thousand pounds of combined frankincense and myrrh moving annually from the Golis Mountain harvesting regions through the inland collection town of Burao and onward, primarily by road, to Somaliland's Berbera port for onward export to buyers across Europe and the Arabian Peninsula, a trade route that in its essential geography, resin harvested in the mountains, collected and consolidated at an inland market town, then exported through the same coastal port that has anchored this specific trade for well over two thousand documented years, represents one of the most genuinely continuous commercial patterns examined anywhere in this book. Before the collapse of the Somali state in the early 1990s, government estimates suggested that roughly ten thousand families across the region depended primarily on frankincense and myrrh resin gathering for their livelihood, a figure that illustrates just how deeply embedded this ancient trade remains within the actual daily economic life of rural communities across northern Somalia, entirely independent of whatever romantic or historical significance outside observers might attach to the substance itself.

One dimension of the contemporary Somaliland resin trade deserves particular attention, because it represents a genuinely distinctive social pattern among the various scent trade conflicts this book has examined. The frankincense and myrrh harvesting and initial sorting economy in Somaliland today employs more women than any other formal industry sector in the territory, according to figures cited by Somaliland's own environment ministry, a demographic pattern that reflects both the specific, labor intensive nature of resin sorting and grading work, which requires the kind of patient, sustained attention that local accounts suggest men in the region are frequently reported as less willing to commit to across the long working days the sorting process demands, and the broader social reality that resin income has become, for many families across rural Somaliland, a genuinely essential and female administered component of household economic survival, with women in the sector widely described, in the assessment of Somaliland's own environment minister, as functioning as the effective breadwinners for their families through their work in the frankincense trade.

The future of this multi thousand year old commercial tradition, remarkably, now faces genuine and serious uncertainty, driven less by the political and administrative conflicts that have shaped so much of this trade's more recent history and more by a set of underlying ecological and geopolitical pressures that threaten the industry's basic sustainability. Somaliland's relative internal stability, a genuine achievement given the chaos that has afflicted southern Somalia across the same decades, exists within a wider regional context that remains, in the assessment of observers tracking the Horn of Africa closely, genuinely precarious, with an unresolved and periodically tense border dispute with Ethiopia and ongoing conflict across the Gulf of Aden in neighboring Yemen creating persistent regional instability risks that could, in a worst case scenario, disrupt the resin trade's established export routes and market access in ways that echo the disruptions colonial administration and subsequent state collapse have already inflicted on this trade across the twentieth century.

Beyond these political and security concerns lies a more fundamental ecological question that connects the frankincense trade directly back to the sustainability challenges already examined in this book's chapters on Mysore sandalwood and Himalayan musk deer. The Boswellia trees that produce frankincense are, like sandalwood, slow growing and vulnerable to overexploitation through excessively frequent or aggressive tapping, and sustained scientific concern has grown in recent years regarding the long term productive capacity of frankincense producing forests across the broader Horn of Africa and Arabian peninsula region, concern rooted in documented evidence that intensive commercial tapping, if not carefully managed and rotated across a tree population to allow adequate recovery time, can measurably reduce both individual tree health and overall seed production, threatening the natural regeneration of frankincense forests even as global demand for the resin, driven substantially by continued and in some markets growing interest from the international perfume, aromatherapy, and wellness industries, shows no sign of meaningfully declining.

What the frankincense and myrrh trade ultimately contributes to this book's broader argument is a demonstration of just how durable a well established scent trade route can prove across even the most extreme and repeated political disruption, surviving the rise and fall of ancient Egyptian dynasties, the deliberate historical obscuring practiced by ancient Arabian intermediary traders, the arrival and eventual departure of British colonial administration, the corrosive centralized mismanagement of a Cold War era military dictatorship, and the subsequent collapse of the state itself into one of the most severe and prolonged instances of national fragmentation anywhere in the late twentieth century world, only to reemerge, in the specific case of Somaliland, as a genuinely functioning, women led export economy still following essentially the same mountain to port geography that Egyptian traders were already exploiting when they sailed south in search of the Land of Punt, more than three thousand years before a single drop of Grasse jasmine oil, Mysore sandalwood, or Bulgarian attar of roses had ever reached a European nose.

CHAPTER EIGHT

The Company That Owned a Smell

On the eighth of May, 1621, a Dutch fleet under the command of a company official named Jan Pieterszoon Coen arrived off a small cluster of volcanic islands in the eastern reaches of what is now Indonesia, carrying sixteen hundred Dutch soldiers, three hundred Javanese convicts, a hundred Japanese mercenary swordsmen, and several hundred enslaved laborers, all committed to a single, narrowly defined commercial objective. The Banda Islands, at that point in world history, were the only place on the entire planet where the nutmeg tree grew, and nutmeg, along with the mace derived from the same fruit, had become one of the most valuable commodities traded anywhere in the world, prized across Europe for its use in cooking, medicine, and, significantly for the purposes of this book, in the perfumery and aromatic preparations of the period, where its warm, sweet, penetrating scent made it a prized ingredient in scented waters, pomanders, and early modern fragrance compounds long before the more familiar culinary spice rack applications that dominate its reputation today. What happened on those islands over the following weeks stands as perhaps the single most brutal example, anywhere in this book, of a chartered trading company using organized, deliberate violence to seize total, permanent control over a fragrant commodity's entire global supply.

The Dutch East India Company, formally chartered in 1602 as an amalgamation of several smaller competing Dutch trading ventures, had spent the better part of two decades before Coen's 1621 expedition attempting to establish exclusive commercial control over Banda's nutmeg trade through negotiated contracts with the Bandanese village elders, known locally as orang kaya, who governed the islands. These negotiations proved persistently unsatisfactory from the Company's perspective. The Bandanese, understandably reluctant to abandon centuries of established trading relationships with English, Portuguese, Chinese, and other Southeast Asian merchants in favor of an exclusive arrangement with a single demanding new European buyer, repeatedly resisted Dutch efforts to enforce the kind of total, contractually guaranteed monopoly the Company's directors in Amsterdam had come to view as essential to protecting the enormous capital investment the enterprise required. When negotiations definitively collapsed following the killing of a Dutch representative during a botched round of talks, the Company's board of directors, known as the Heeren Zeventien, had already concluded, years earlier in 1614, that force would ultimately be required to secure the monopoly they wanted, a decision Coen, upon his appointment as governor general of the Dutch East Indies in 1617 and 1618, was entirely prepared to carry out.

Coen's own stated philosophy, preserved in his surviving correspondence with the Company's directors, leaves remarkably little room for ambiguity about the methods he considered acceptable in pursuit of commercial monopoly. In a letter that has become one of the most frequently cited documents in the historiography of Dutch colonial violence, Coen urged the Company's leadership not to despair and not to spare their enemies, asserting his confidence that nothing in the world could hinder the Company's ambitions because, in his own explicit framing, God was on their side. This was not merely rhetorical flourish. When Coen's expedition landed on the main Banda islands in 1621, the resulting campaign, executed with the systematic thoroughness of a man who genuinely believed his commercial objectives carried something close to divine sanction, resulted in the deaths of approximately twenty eight hundred Bandanese people, alongside the enslavement of a further seventeen hundred, out of a total pre invasion population that most historical estimates place at somewhere between fifteen and twenty thousand people spread across the archipelago. Coen personally presided over what amounted to show trials of forty four captured Bandanese village leaders, all of whom were subsequently executed, and the broader campaign of killing, forced deportation, starvation, and disease that followed left the islands so severely depopulated that later historians and, in the twenty first century, the government of independent Indonesia itself, have come to characterize the episode as an act of genocide, a word not used lightly or often in the broader historical literature covering European colonial trading company violence.

The commercial logic underlying this catastrophic human cost was, in the Company's own internal accounting, entirely coherent. With the Bandanese population eliminated or enslaved, the Dutch East India Company redistributed the nutmeg growing land among Dutch plantation owners, known as perkeniers, who were required to sell their entire nutmeg and mace harvest exclusively to the Company at fixed, Company determined prices, while importing enslaved labor from Java to actually work the plantations under conditions that surviving records describe as severe, with correspondingly short average life expectancy among the enslaved workforce. This arrangement gave the Dutch East India Company what amounted to a genuinely total, planet wide monopoly over the global nutmeg supply, a monopoly so complete and so tightly held that it remained essentially unbroken for well over a century, surviving intact until the collapse of the Company itself amid the broader upheaval of the French Revolutionary Wars at the very end of the eighteenth century. For roughly a hundred and eighty years, in other words, a single European trading company, having secured its position through one of the most brutal single episodes of colonial violence in the entire early modern period, controlled the world's entire commercial supply of a fragrant, valuable natural commodity, an achievement in monopoly control that even Tipu Sultan's sandalwood decree, examined earlier in this book, never came close to matching in absolute completeness, if only because sandalwood, unlike Banda's nutmeg trees before European transplantation efforts eventually succeeded elsewhere, was never confined to quite so small and conquerable a patch of geography.

Coen's reward for the Banda massacre, it is worth noting plainly, was not censure but professional advancement and the continued confidence of his Company superiors in Amsterdam, whose primary concern, based on the surviving record of their internal deliberations, centered overwhelmingly on the security of the nutmeg monopoly Coen had delivered rather than on the human cost of delivering it. This response, a chartered commercial company effectively rewarding a colonial governor for extreme violence deployed in pursuit of monopoly control over a fragrant commodity, establishes a template that recurs, in less extreme but structurally comparable form, across nearly every chapter of this book. Whether the mechanism was a royal decree in eighteenth century Mysore, a guild charter in early modern Grasse, or a colonial governor general's military campaign in seventeenth century Indonesia, the underlying pattern remains remarkably consistent: whoever controls the ground where a scarce, internationally valuable fragrant material grows can convert that geographic control into a species of political power that operates according to its own logic, often only loosely constrained by whatever formal legal or moral framework nominally governs the broader territory in question.

The English East India Company, the Dutch Company's principal commercial rival throughout this period, pursued a broadly similar strategy of aggressive monopoly seeking across the South and East Asian trade routes it contested with the Dutch, though the English Company's specific territorial ambitions gravitated more heavily toward the Indian subcontinent following its comparative defeat in the direct competition for the more tightly confined Spice Island nutmeg and clove trade that the Dutch ultimately secured almost entirely for themselves. Chartered in 1600 under Queen Elizabeth the First with an initial monopoly on English trade throughout the region east of the Cape of Good Hope, the English Company began as a straightforward commercial venture focused on securing spices, silk, and other valuable Asian goods for the English market, only gradually acquiring the territorial and military dimensions that would eventually transform it into something closer to a private government ruling over vast stretches of the Indian subcontinent. By the mid eighteenth century, the Company's growing military capability, combined with the political vacuum created by the accelerating decline of Mughal imperial authority across India, allowed it to begin acquiring direct territorial control rather than simply negotiating trading rights with independent local rulers, a transition most decisively marked by its victory at the Battle of Plassey in 1757, which established effective Company control over the wealthy province of Bengal and set the pattern for the following century of expanding Company territorial rule across the subcontinent.

It was within this broader context of expanding Company territorial authority that the sandalwood monopoly examined in an earlier chapter of this book found its way into Company hands, following the defeat and death of Tipu Sultan in 1799. As already discussed, the East India Company, upon assuming effective political control over the restored Mysore kingdom under the Wadiyar dynasty, chose to preserve rather than dismantle the sandalwood monopoly Tipu Sultan had originally established as a wartime revenue measure against the very Company that now inherited it, a decision that illustrates with particular clarity just how readily a colonial trading company, whatever its stated commercial and political philosophy, would preserve an existing fragrant commodity monopoly when the alternative meant sacrificing a reliable revenue stream. The Company that had spent decades fighting Tipu Sultan across four separate wars had no ideological objection whatsoever to continuing his sandalwood policy once his kingdom, and the tax revenue that policy generated, had become its own.

This pattern, colonial and quasi governmental trading companies inheriting, adapting, and in some cases dramatically intensifying pre existing local commodity control systems rather than replacing them with something genuinely new, recurs across the broader history of European commercial expansion into Asia and appears in variant forms wherever chartered companies encountered fragrant or otherwise valuable natural resources already subject to some form of pre existing local or regional control. The specific mechanisms varied considerably by territory and by company, ranging from the outright genocidal violence Coen employed at Banda, to the somewhat less extreme but still coercive contract enforcement the Dutch Company pursued elsewhere across the Spice Islands, to the English Company's more gradual, negotiated absorption of existing revenue systems including Mysore's sandalwood monopoly, but the underlying commercial logic connecting these varied approaches remained remarkably consistent throughout: a chartered trading company, backed by private capital and increasingly by its own independent military capability, sought to convert control over a geographically concentrated, internationally valuable natural resource into the kind of durable, defensible monopoly position that would generate reliable returns for its investors across decades or, in the Dutch Company's Banda nutmeg case, close to two centuries of continuous operation.

The broader economic significance of this company driven monopoly model to European state finances by the height of its operation was genuinely enormous, extending well beyond the direct commercial profits captured by company shareholders. By the late eighteenth century, tax revenue collected by the English East India Company from its expanding Indian territories had grown to represent close to ten percent of Britain's entire national tax revenue, a figure that illustrates just how thoroughly the fortunes of a nominally private trading company had, by this point, become interwoven with the broader fiscal health of the British state itself. This intertwining of private commercial interest and national state finance created powerful institutional incentives, extending well beyond the immediate commercial ambitions of company merchants and colonial administrators on the ground, to preserve and defend whatever profitable resource monopolies a company had managed to establish, since the revenue generated increasingly underwrote not merely shareholder dividends but a meaningful share of the parent nation's own governmental operations.

The eventual unwinding of these company commodity monopolies, when it finally came, arrived not primarily through moral reconsideration of the violence and coercion that had established them in the first place, but through the more mundane forces of shifting metropolitan politics and changing commercial circumstance. The British Parliament formally stripped the English East India Company of its trading monopoly in 1813, following decades of mounting domestic criticism, much of it grounded less in humanitarian concern for colonized populations than in the frustration of rival British merchants excluded from the lucrative Asian trade the Company had long monopolized for itself. The Company's remaining administrative and governmental functions in India persisted for several further decades, until the major rebellion of 1857, known variously as the Indian Mutiny or the First War of Independence depending on the historical perspective from which it is described, prompted the British government to dissolve the Company's political authority entirely and assume direct Crown control over its Indian territories, formally inaugurating the period of direct British colonial rule in India that would persist until Indian independence in 1947. The Dutch East India Company met an even more abrupt institutional end, collapsing amid the financial and military pressures of the French Revolutionary Wars in 1799, its various territorial possessions across the East Indies eventually absorbed into direct administration by the Dutch state itself.

What both companies left behind, in territories stretching from the Banda Islands to the sandalwood forests of Mysore, were commodity control systems, tax structures, and administrative precedents that frequently persisted, in modified but recognizable form, well beyond the specific commercial entities that had originally established them, exactly as this book has already documented in the specific case of Mysore sandalwood policy surviving, largely intact in its essential structure, across the transition from Tipu Sultan's kingdom through Company rule, British Crown rule, and ultimately into independent India's own state administration. The fragrant commodities these companies fought, negotiated, and in the most extreme case committed mass killing to control did not disappear once the companies themselves dissolved. They simply passed, monopoly structure largely intact, into the hands of whatever government inherited administrative authority over the territory where they grew, a pattern of institutional continuity across radically different political systems that stands as one of the more genuinely underappreciated legacies of the entire chartered company era of European colonial expansion.

There is a final, sobering point worth making explicitly before this chapter closes, one that connects directly back to the book's broader argument about scent trades and the political power they generate. The Banda Islands today remain, in global terms, a genuinely minor commercial nutmeg producer, having lost their historical monopoly position once successful transplantation efforts, pursued deliberately by rival European powers eager to break the Dutch stranglehold on the trade, eventually established viable nutmeg cultivation in other tropical locations including Grenada in the Caribbean, which today produces a substantial share of the world's nutmeg supply from trees descended from seedlings smuggled out of the Dutch monopoly zone in the decades following Coen's conquest. The monopoly that had seemed, to the Company directors who rewarded Coen's brutality with continued confidence and career advancement, permanently secure through the elimination of an entire indigenous population, ultimately proved no more durable than any other artificial scarcity examined in this book, undone in the end not by moral reconsideration or colonial reform but by the same relentless commercial logic that had created it in the first place: somewhere, eventually, someone else always finds a way to grow the tree.

CHAPTER NINE

Perfumers at War

This book opened in the hills above Cannes, tracing how a town's need to disguise the smell of rotting leather grew, across four centuries, into the world's dominant perfume industry, an industry powerful enough to shape the political fortunes of provincial administrators sent to govern the region on behalf of Paris. It is fitting, then, to return to Grasse before this book's final chapters carry the reader into the more recent past, because the twentieth century delivered to Grasse's perfume trade a set of challenges that none of its earlier provincial rivalries had prepared it for, challenges that arrived not from a competing perfume house or a disgruntled grower but from world war, occupation, industrial chemistry, and, in the final and in some ways most decisive blow, simple real estate economics.

At the height of its natural flower production, sometime around the middle of the twentieth century, the broader Pays de Grasse region supported an extraordinary concentration of dedicated perfume agriculture, with family growers cultivating close to five thousand acres of flowers and aromatic plants specifically for the fragrance trade, a total that included roughly two thousand acres devoted to jasmine alone, seventeen hundred acres of the specific centifolia rose variety known locally as the May rose, and a further hundred and sixty acres given over to tuberose, alongside smaller plantings of orange blossom, violet, verbena, and the other aromatic botanicals that had made the region's reputation. This was industrial scale floriculture organized entirely around the needs of a single downstream industry, a scale of dedicated cultivation that reflected decades of accumulated agricultural investment and technical refinement, and it represented, at its peak, one of the most concentrated and economically significant single crop agricultural systems anywhere in France.

The Second World War brought disruption to this system on a scale the industry had never previously experienced, even accounting for the earlier convulsions of the French Revolution and the various nineteenth century tax and trade disputes examined in this book's opening chapter. Southern France came under direct German military occupation in November 1942, following the earlier period of nominal autonomy under the collaborationist Vichy government that had administered the unoccupied southern zone since France's defeat in 1940, and the war years that followed placed severe strain on every dimension of Grasse's carefully calibrated agricultural and industrial system. Labor shortages, as young men across the region were conscripted into forced labor programs or otherwise removed from the local workforce, made the kind of intensive, time sensitive hand harvesting that jasmine and rose cultivation demanded increasingly difficult to sustain at anything approaching prewar scale. Fuel and transportation shortages disrupted the movement of both raw flowers and finished perfume products to markets that, in ordinary peacetime conditions, had depended heavily on rapid, reliable transport given the perishable nature of fresh flower material and the international character of the finished perfume trade's customer base.

Perhaps more significantly for the industry's longer term trajectory, the general economic dislocation of the occupation years accelerated a trend that would define Grasse's perfume trade for the remainder of the twentieth century: growing dependence on synthetic and imported raw materials as a hedge against the increasing unreliability and cost of purely local, natural flower cultivation. The war years, whatever their immediate human and economic hardship, in some respects previewed a structural transformation that had already begun taking shape in the industry before 1939 and that would accelerate dramatically in the postwar decades, as advancing organic chemistry made it increasingly possible to synthesize convincing approximations of natural floral scents in a laboratory, at a small fraction of the cost, and without any dependence whatsoever on the narrow seasonal harvest windows, unpredictable weather, and intensive hand labor that had defined natural flower cultivation in the Grasse hills for the previous three centuries.

The postwar decades brought a genuine golden age for Grasse's perfume industry in terms of its cultural prestige and international commercial reach, even as the underlying economics of natural flower cultivation within the region began a long, largely irreversible decline. It was in Grasse, and specifically through the collaboration between the couturier Gabrielle Chanel and the French Russian perfumer Ernest Beaux, that one of the most commercially and culturally significant fragrances in modern history had already emerged in the years just before the war, when Chanel No. 5 launched in 1921, built around an unprecedented, heavy use of synthetic aldehyde compounds layered with substantial quantities of authentic Grasse jasmine and May rose absolute, a formula that would establish both a new aesthetic direction for modern perfumery and a template, blending expensive natural materials with cost effective synthetic innovation, that the broader industry would increasingly follow across the following decades. This subject, the specific chemical revolution that aldehydes and other early synthetic compounds represented, and the industry wide transformation it set in motion, merits its own extended treatment in the chapter that follows this one.

For Grasse specifically, the relevant twentieth century story is less about any single celebrated fragrance and more about the sustained, structural pressure that cheaper synthetic alternatives placed on the economics of natural flower farming across the postwar decades. Beginning in the 1960s and accelerating through the 1970s, large international chemical conglomerates began acquiring processing facilities within Grasse itself, bringing with them access to an increasingly rich and varied palette of synthetic aromatic molecules offered at prices that natural flower cultivation, constrained by its narrow seasonal harvest windows and continued dependence on increasingly expensive hand labor, simply could not match on a purely cost competitive basis. This shift did not eliminate demand for genuine Grasse grown natural materials, which retained, and to a considerable extent still retain today, a premium reputation among the world's most prestigious perfume houses precisely because of qualities, complexity, subtlety, the specific character that terroir and traditional processing methods impart, that synthetic reproduction, however chemically sophisticated, has never fully replicated. But it dramatically reduced the sheer acreage of land that remained economically viable to dedicate to natural perfume flower cultivation, as growers increasingly found more profitable uses for their land than continuing to compete against synthetic alternatives on the lower end of the fragrance ingredient market.

This economic pressure combined, through the same postwar decades, with an entirely separate and in some respects even more consequential threat to the region's agricultural land: the extraordinary postwar tourism and real estate boom that transformed the neighboring French Riviera, the Côte d'Azur, into one of the most valuable coastal property markets anywhere in the world. Land in and around Grasse that had, for three centuries, been valued primarily according to its suitability for jasmine and rose cultivation suddenly found itself valued according to an entirely different calculus, one measured in villa construction potential and proximity to the glamorous coastal resort towns of Cannes, Nice, and Antibes that drew wealthy visitors, and increasingly wealthy permanent residents, from across Europe and beyond. Faced with the choice between the continued, increasingly marginal returns of natural flower cultivation and the often dramatically more lucrative option of selling agricultural land for residential development, the great majority of Grasse's historical flower growing families made the economically rational choice to sell.

The resulting decline in cultivated acreage, when measured against the industry's mid twentieth century peak, has been genuinely dramatic. Where the broader Pays de Grasse region once supported some five thousand acres of dedicated perfume flower cultivation, contemporary figures place the town's own jasmine cultivation at roughly a dozen acres and its rose cultivation at somewhere in the neighborhood of a hundred and twenty acres, a contraction of well over ninety percent from the industry's historical peak, even as the broader Grasse perfume industry as a whole, encompassing processing, formulation, and the corporate headquarters of internationally significant fragrance houses, has continued to thrive and, in recent decades, has experienced a genuine renaissance in cultural prestige and international recognition, culminating in Grasse's formal recognition by UNESCO in 2018, when the organization inscribed the region's traditional perfume making knowledge, techniques, and practices on its Representative List of the Intangible Cultural Heritage of Humanity, a designation that explicitly celebrates the specialized agricultural and artisanal expertise Grasse has preserved even as the raw acreage supporting that expertise has contracted to a small fraction of its historical extent.

A handful of growing families, most prominently the multi generational Mul family, whose cultivation of May rose and jasmine for use in Chanel No. 5 and other prestige fragrances has continued across five generations, held onto their land through the decades of postwar contraction, choosing to continue natural flower cultivation even as the great majority of their neighbors sold out to developers, and it is largely through the continued commitment of families like these that Grasse's living natural flower cultivation tradition survives today at all, rather than existing purely as a historical memory preserved in museum exhibits and heritage designations. These surviving growers today typically operate under long term, often multi decade supply contracts with specific luxury perfume houses, arrangements that guarantee both a stable market for their harvest and a price premium reflecting the authentic Grasse provenance that remains, even in an era of sophisticated synthetic alternatives, a genuine and commercially significant point of differentiation for the world's most prestigious fragrance brands. A kilogram of genuine Grasse jasmine absolute today commands a price that can exceed fifty thousand euros, a figure that illustrates just how dramatically the economics of the trade have shifted from the industry's nineteenth century peak, when jasmine was processed by the literal ton across hundreds of small family farms, toward a twenty first century model built around a small number of highly specialized, contractually secured growers supplying an increasingly rarefied luxury market.

Chanel itself took the unusual step, beginning in 1987, of entering into an exclusive supply agreement directly with the Mul family, an arrangement later formalized through Chanel's own direct acquisition of the family's growing fields, a vertical integration strategy that guarantees the house permanent, contractually secure access to the specific jasmine and May rose fields that have supplied its signature fragrance for decades, insulating at least this single, historically significant supply relationship from the broader market pressures of shifting land values and competing synthetic alternatives that have driven the great majority of Grasse's other historical flower growers out of the trade entirely. Other prestige houses, watching Chanel's example, have pursued broadly comparable direct land ownership or long term exclusive contract strategies with the region's remaining flower growers in the years since, a pattern that has itself become a genuinely significant factor helping stabilize what little natural flower cultivation acreage remains within the immediate Grasse area, even as it has simultaneously concentrated control over that shrinking acreage into the hands of an increasingly small number of major international luxury conglomerates, a considerable structural change from the more fragmented, independent family farming pattern that had characterized the trade across its previous three centuries of history.

There is a specific irony worth noting in this transformation, one that connects Grasse's twentieth century story back to the broader argument this book has been developing across its opening chapters. The economic and political leverage that Grasse's perfume houses accumulated over provincial administrators during the eighteenth and nineteenth centuries rested fundamentally on the sheer scale of the local agricultural economy the perfume trade commanded, thousands of acres under cultivation, an entire regional workforce oriented around the flower harvest calendar, and a correspondingly large tax base that provincial officials could not afford to alienate. The Grasse of the twenty first century, however culturally prestigious and however commercially successful its remaining perfume houses and processing facilities continue to be, no longer commands anything close to that scale of direct agricultural economic weight within the surrounding region. Its political leverage today rests instead on brand value, heritage tourism, and the specific prestige UNESCO recognition and continued association with the world's most famous perfume brands confer, a form of soft power considerably different in character from the raw agricultural economic muscle that had allowed nineteenth century Grasse perfumers to quietly stall unfavorable tax proposals and shape departmental infrastructure spending in earlier decades.

It is worth pausing on what daily commercial life actually looked like within Grasse's perfume trade during the occupation years specifically, because the pattern that emerged there echoes, in a distinctly French wartime register, the black market dynamics this book has already documented in very different contexts, from Mysore's illegal sandalwood networks to the deliberately obscured Arabian intermediary trade in ancient Somali frankincense. Wartime price controls and rationing, imposed across occupied and Vichy administered France alike as part of the broader effort to direct scarce resources toward the German war economy, applied in principle to agricultural production of every kind, including the flower harvests that fed Grasse's perfume houses. In practice, as with rationed goods across occupied Europe, a parallel unofficial market inevitably emerged alongside the official, price controlled one, and Grasse's long established networks of growers, brokers, and perfume house buyers, relationships built up over generations of peacetime trading, proved just as capable of adapting to wartime scarcity and improvised black market exchange as they had previously proven capable of navigating nineteenth century tax disputes and departmental politics. Perfume, unlike food, was never going to be treated as a genuine wartime priority by an occupying administration focused overwhelmingly on extracting raw materials and labor useful to its military effort, which left Grasse's trade in a strange, liminal position throughout the occupation: neither fully suppressed nor fully protected, operating in the gaps of an administrative system with far more urgent concerns than the fate of a French luxury export industry.

The industry's recovery in the years immediately following liberation was neither instantaneous nor uniform across the region's various growers and houses. Some family operations, particularly those that had maintained continuity of land ownership and cultivation know how through the war years despite reduced output, were positioned to resume something close to normal production relatively quickly once wartime disruptions to labor, fuel, and transport eased. Others, particularly smaller operations that had been forced to abandon cultivation entirely during the most difficult years of the occupation, found the specialized agricultural knowledge and the multi year investment required to bring fields back into full flowering production a genuinely difficult barrier to reentry, one that likely contributed, alongside the separate and larger economic pressures from synthetic competition and coastal real estate values already discussed, to the broader postwar contraction in the number of families actively engaged in natural flower cultivation across the region.

The war years themselves, and the broader mid twentieth century pressures that followed them, thus mark a genuine turning point in this book's larger narrative, the moment at which the oldest and, in many respects, most historically influential of all the scent trade centers examined in these pages began the transition from a raw materials economy commanding direct political leverage over the territory that produced it, toward something closer to a heritage and brand economy, one that retains real commercial and cultural significance but that operates according to a fundamentally different logic than the land intensive, labor intensive, harvest calendar driven economic system that had defined Grasse, and had shaped the political fortunes of the officials sent to govern it, for the preceding three and a half centuries. The chapters that remain in this book will trace how other scent trades, facing broadly comparable pressure from synthetic chemistry, changing consumer preference, and shifting global supply chains, navigated, or in some cases failed to navigate, this same essential transition from raw material power to something else entirely, a transition whose final chapter, for several of the commodities this book has already examined, remains genuinely unwritten even today.

CHAPTER TEN

The Chemists' Rebellion

Every conflict examined so far in this book shares a common structural premise: a fragrant material grows, or is secreted, or washes ashore, in one specific, geographically limited place, and whoever controls that place controls the trade. The nineteenth century brought a slow moving but ultimately devastating challenge to this premise, one that arrived not from a rival monarch, a colonial governor, or a rebellious mountain bandit, but from a laboratory bench. Organic chemistry, developing rapidly across Germany, France, and Britain through the middle and later decades of the nineteenth century, began proving something that no perfumer, however skilled, and no monopolist, however ruthless, had ever previously had to seriously reckon with: that many of the specific chemical compounds responsible for a natural material's characteristic scent could, once properly identified and understood, be synthesized directly in a laboratory, without any flower, any tree, any animal gland, or any accident of geography whatsoever standing between the raw chemical precursors and the finished, recognizable fragrance.

The opening moves in this quiet revolution arrived earlier than most people assume. Coumarin, the sweet, almond and fresh cut hay scented compound that gives tonka beans their distinctive fragrance, was first isolated from the natural bean by the German chemist August Vogel in 1820, but it was the English chemist William Henry Perkin who, in 1868, first achieved its full synthetic production from simpler chemical precursors, decades before perfumers began seriously incorporating the synthetic version into finished fragrances. Vanillin followed a similar trajectory, first isolated as a crystalline compound from actual vanilla pods in 1858, before German chemists Wilhelm Haarmann and Ferdinand Tiemann achieved industrial scale synthetic production in 1876, working from the glycosides present in ordinary pine tree sap rather than from vanilla plants grown anywhere in the tropics. The commercial consequences of this second breakthrough arrived quickly and severely. Contemporary accounts of the period describe the sudden availability of cheap synthetic vanillin as having triggered a genuine economic depression within the natural vanilla growing industry, an early and instructive preview of the disruption that synthetic chemistry would repeatedly visit upon natural fragrant material producers across the following century and a half.

This pattern, a natural material's price collapsing once chemists successfully identified and synthesized its key aromatic compound, would recur with remarkable regularity across the following decades, and nowhere more dramatically than with musk. In 1888, the German chemist Albert Baur, working not on perfumery at all but attempting to develop more effective explosives, accidentally discovered a synthetic compound possessing a distinctly musk like fragrance, a substance that came to be known as Musk Baur, followed in 1894 by a further synthetic musk compound called Musk Ketone that would remain in widespread commercial use for the following century, only being phased out amid environmental and safety concerns beginning in the 1990s. The commercial and, in an important sense, the conservation significance of this discovery is difficult to overstate. Natural musk, extracted through the killing of Himalayan musk deer as documented in an earlier chapter of this book, had been for most of recorded history an essentially irreplaceable perfumery ingredient, one whose scarcity and lethal extraction method drove exactly the kind of black market poaching economy this book has already traced in considerable detail. Baur's accidental discovery offered, for the first time in the entire multi thousand year history of musk in perfumery, a genuine, chemically distinct alternative that did not require killing a single animal, and contemporary industry sources from the period explicitly describe the newly available synthetic option as considerably less expensive than genuine Tonkin musk, the specific grade of natural deer musk that had, prior to this discovery, dominated the highest end of the trade, with natural Tonkin musk itself becoming subject to increasing prohibition in the years that followed as synthetic alternatives proved commercially viable.

The broader pattern of synthetic discovery accelerated rapidly through the final decades of the nineteenth century and into the opening years of the twentieth, with chemists across Europe successfully isolating and then synthesizing an expanding range of compounds responsible for specific, recognizable natural scents. Heliotropin, discovered in 1869, offered perfumers access to the sweet, powdery fragrance of the heliotrope flower. Ionone, synthesized by the chemists Ferdinand Tiemann and Paul Kruger in 1898, provided an economical, chemically stable approximation of the delicate, notoriously difficult to extract scent of violets, a flower whose natural essential oil had always been prohibitively expensive to produce at any meaningful commercial scale given the extraordinarily low yield of usable fragrant material any given quantity of violet blossoms actually contained. Isobutyl quinoline, synthesized by the Czech chemist Zdenko Hans Skraup in 1880, gave perfumers access to a convincing, laboratory produced leather note that could anchor an entire new category of leather themed fragrances without requiring the kind of genuine animal hide extracts that earlier perfumers had relied upon, extracts whose supply chain connected uncomfortably close to the same tanning industry whose foul smell had originally launched Grasse's perfume trade three centuries earlier, as this book's opening chapter described.

No single figure embodies the commercial opportunity this synthetic revolution created more clearly than François Coty, a Corsican born entrepreneur who trained briefly at the House of Chiris in Grasse before launching his own perfume business in the opening years of the twentieth century, and whose career trajectory illustrates with particular clarity how synthetic chemistry fundamentally reshaped the competitive economics of the entire fragrance industry. Coty's early fragrances built deliberately and prominently around the new synthetic materials becoming available to perfumers of his generation. His 1905 fragrance L'Origan incorporated the synthetic compounds Iralia and Diantine alongside natural orange blossom, violet, jasmine, rose, and carnation, while his 1917 fragrance Chypre, following an established style pioneered by the rival house of Guerlain, built its distinctive accord around a combination of natural oakmoss, patchouli, jasmine, vetiver, sandalwood, and bergamot together with synthetic vanillin and coumarin, a formula whose specific combination of ingredients would go on to define an entire enduring category, the chypre fragrance family, that continues to shape perfumery classification more than a century later.

Coty's commercial philosophy, by his own explicit self description, treated the emerging science of synthetic aroma chemistry not as a threat to genuine perfumery craft but as an essential creative and commercial tool, a perspective he apparently considered sufficiently central to his professional identity that he reportedly listed himself, across the various titles printed on his business card, as artist, industrialist, technician, economist, financier, and sociologist all at once, a self characterization that captures, with a certain immodest precision, exactly how thoroughly the synthetic chemistry revolution had begun blurring the traditional boundary between perfumer as artisan and perfumer as industrial chemist and businessman. Coty's commercial success, building an internationally significant perfume house substantially on the back of accessible, affordably priced fragrances that incorporated synthetic materials as a matter of core creative and commercial strategy rather than embarrassed necessity, demonstrated decisively to the broader industry that synthetic chemistry offered a genuine path to commercial success rather than representing, as more traditionally minded perfumers of the period sometimes characterized it, a debasement of authentic perfumery craft.

The most historically celebrated single demonstration of synthetic chemistry's creative potential arrived in 1921, when the French Russian chemist and perfumer Ernest Beaux, working with the couturier Gabrielle Chanel on what would become Chanel No. 5, incorporated an unprecedentedly heavy concentration of synthetic aldehyde compounds into the finished fragrance, reportedly after an assistant accidentally added a far higher dose of aldehydes to one test sample than

Beaux himself had originally intended, a genuine happy accident that Chanel, upon smelling the resulting sample, immediately recognized as something genuinely novel rather than a formulation error to be corrected and discarded. The finished fragrance combined this aldehyde overdose with substantial quantities of authentic natural jasmine and May rose absolute sourced from Grasse, alongside natural civet, musk, and sandalwood in its base notes, creating a formula that balanced expensive, prestige signaling natural materials against a genuinely innovative synthetic backbone that gave the finished perfume a distinctive, almost sparkling quality that natural materials alone could never have achieved. The commercial and cultural success of Chanel No. 5 in the decades that followed, becoming what remains, over a century after its 1921 launch, among the most commercially successful and culturally recognized fragrances ever created, offered the entire perfume industry an unmistakable demonstration that synthetic and natural materials, deployed together with sufficient creative skill, could achieve results neither category could realistically achieve alone.

The pace of synthetic discovery continued accelerating across the middle decades of the twentieth century, driven by the broader, rapid advancement of organic chemistry as an academic and industrial discipline across this period, and particularly by the dramatic postwar expansion of the petrochemical industry, which provided both the raw chemical feedstocks and the industrial infrastructure necessary to manufacture aroma chemicals at genuinely massive commercial scale and correspondingly low cost. Industry historians of synthetic perfumery materials generally identify the 1950s as the specific decade in which synthetic aroma chemical development truly accelerated into full industrial maturity, a shift driven directly by the practical limitations inherent in natural essential oil production, limitations this book has now documented extensively across its chapters on sandalwood, rose, jasmine, musk, and ambergris, limitations involving narrow seasonal harvest windows, unpredictable weather and crop yields, geographically constrained growing regions vulnerable to political disruption, and, in several of the cases this book has examined, outright species level ecological collapse driven by unsustainable extraction.

What synthetic chemistry offered the fragrance industry, in other words, was not merely a cost advantage, though the cost advantage was often genuinely enormous, but something closer to a fundamental structural solution to nearly every specific vulnerability this book has documented across its preceding chapters. A synthetic musk compound could not be threatened by CITES trade restrictions targeting endangered musk deer populations, because it required no deer at all. A synthetic sandalwood approximation could not be caught up in a violent thirty year forest war between an armed bandit and two Indian state governments, because it required no sandalwood forest, no thirty to sixty year tree maturation cycle, and no state monopoly to enforce. A synthetic jasmine or rose compound could not be disrupted by a narrow, weather dependent harvest window measured in weeks, because it could, in principle, be manufactured continuously, at consistent quality, in any properly equipped chemical plant located anywhere in the world with access to the necessary industrial feedstocks, entirely independent of season, climate, or the specific geology and microclimate of any particular valley or hillside.

This is, in the most literal sense possible, a genuine rebellion against the entire economic and political logic this book has spent its preceding chapters documenting, a rebellion waged not with muskets or paramilitary task forces but with laboratory glassware, patent filings, and industrial chemistry, and it succeeded, to a very substantial degree, in doing exactly what its name implies: breaking, or at minimum severely weakening, the specific geographic monopolies that had for centuries allowed control over a particular patch of land, forest, or coastline to translate into outsized political and economic power. The rulers, colonial governors, guild masters, and forest bandits examined throughout this book had all, in their different ways, built their power on the fundamental scarcity and geographic specificity of a fragrant natural resource. Synthetic chemistry attacked that scarcity directly, offering, compound by compound, molecule by molecule, alternative pathways to many of the same scents that had previously required control over an actual physical place on the actual physical earth.

It would be a significant overstatement, however, to conclude that synthetic chemistry simply ended the scent trade conflicts this book has documented, and the ongoing, present day realities of sandalwood smuggling, musk deer poaching, and ambergris black markets, all examined in their own dedicated chapters, demonstrate clearly that no such clean resolution has actually occurred. Synthetic alternatives, however sophisticated, have consistently proven better at approximating the character of a natural scent than at fully replicating its complete, often extraordinarily complex chemical composition, and the most demanding, prestige oriented segment of the global perfume market has, across more than a century of advancing synthetic chemistry, continued to place a significant premium on genuine natural materials specifically because of qualities, depth, complexity, the countless trace compounds a single natural essential oil actually contains beyond whatever single molecule chemists have managed to isolate and name, that synthetic reproduction has never fully matched. This persistent demand for authentic natural material, even at prices that can reach tens of thousands of euros per kilogram for the finest Grasse jasmine absolute, has kept the underlying economic incentives driving nearly every conflict examined in this book alive and functioning, even as synthetic chemistry has simultaneously and genuinely transformed the broader, mass market segment of the fragrance industry, making perfume, in the assessment of numerous industry historians, into a genuinely accessible mass consumer product for the first time in its multi thousand year history, rather than remaining an exclusive luxury reserved for those wealthy enough to afford natural materials extracted at enormous cost from forests, flower fields, and ocean beaches scattered across half the globe.

The chemists' rebellion, in the end, proved to be neither a complete victory nor a complete failure, but something more genuinely interesting and considerably more relevant to this book's broader argument: a partial, permanent restructuring of the underlying economics of scent, one that peeled away the enormous mass market for affordable, everyday fragrance from the older, narrower, but still genuinely lucrative and still genuinely violence prone market for prestige natural materials, a market that continues, even now, in the second quarter of the twenty first century, to sustain smuggling networks, black markets, species level conservation crises, and the occasional armed conflict between state authorities and the individuals determined to profit from whatever fragrant scarcity remains.

CHAPTER ELEVEN

The Soap That Broke a State

This book has already traced how Tipu Sultan's 1792 declaration of sandalwood as a royal tree, and the state monopoly it established, survived the fall of his kingdom, the century of British colonial administration that followed, and the violent three decade career of the bandit Veerappan, whose war against that monopoly's enforcement mechanisms claimed close to two hundred lives before his death in a 2004 ambush. What that earlier account left largely unexamined is the specific institutional descendant of Tipu Sultan's original monopoly that exists today, a state owned soap manufacturer whose brand has become so thoroughly woven into regional identity that a 2026 marketing decision involving its choice of celebrity brand ambassador triggered a genuine political controversy within the Karnataka state government, more than two centuries after a defeated eighteenth century ruler first declared the tree that supplies its signature ingredient the property of the crown.

The specific institution in question, Karnataka Soaps and Detergents Limited, traces its own organizational origins to 1916, when Krishna Raja Wadiyar the Fourth, the reigning Maharaja of Mysore under British colonial oversight, established a Government Soap Factory on the outskirts of Bangalore with the explicit purpose of processing a specific and, at the time, genuinely urgent economic problem: a surplus of sandalwood oil that had accumulated as a direct consequence of a collapse in Western export demand following the disruption of international trade during the First World War. Rather than allowing this surplus to sit unused, the Maharaja's administration, working with the engineering expertise of the distinguished Indian civil engineer and statesman M. Visvesvaraya, who served as the kingdom's Diwan or chief minister during this period, converted what had been a purely raw material export business into a finished consumer product manufacturing operation, launching the soap that would become known as Mysore Sandal Soap in 1918, a product built directly around the specific, distinctive fragrance of authentic sandalwood oil sourced from the same state controlled forests that had operated under a royal monopoly since Tipu Sultan's original 1792 decree.

The soap proved to be a genuinely inspired commercial adaptation of the underlying monopoly resource, transforming a raw material subject to volatile international export markets into a finished consumer good with a distinctive, defensible brand identity that no foreign competitor could realistically replicate, since no other soap manufacturer anywhere in the world possessed comparable legal access to genuine Mysore sandalwood oil at anything approaching the same scale or cost. Over the following decades, the soap became genuinely iconic within Indian consumer culture, its distinctive oval shape and its authentic sandalwood fragrance earning it a reputation for quality and authenticity that survived India's transition from princely state administration through independence and into the modern era of Karnataka state governance, with the operation formally reorganized as a limited liability corporation named Karnataka Soaps and Detergents Limited in 1980, when the government merged the original Mysore facility with an additional sandalwood oil processing unit operating in Shivamogga.

In the decades since this 1980 reorganization, the company has expanded its product range well beyond the original bar soap into a broader portfolio that today includes sandalwood incense sticks, talcum powder, hair oil, and a range of cosmetic products, alongside continued production of the pure sandalwood oil itself as a standalone export commodity sold directly to international perfume houses and other industrial buyers, a diversification strategy that reflects the broader industry wide shift, documented throughout this book, toward extracting maximum commercial value from an increasingly scarce and expensive raw material rather than relying on volume alone. The company today operates its manufacturing facilities primarily at Mysuru and Shivamogga, maintaining a workforce whose institutional memory and specialized processing expertise, passed down across multiple generations of employees in a manner not entirely unlike the accumulated craft knowledge this book's opening chapters described among the flower growers of Grasse, represents its own form of accumulated value that has proven considerably harder for the company's leaner private sector competitors to replicate than the underlying sandalwood oil supply itself.

The commercial logic underlying this entire operation, and the reason it merits inclusion as a distinct chapter in this book rather than simply as a footnote to the earlier discussion of Tipu Sultan's original monopoly, rests on a specific legal and economic mechanism that connects directly back through more than two centuries of continuous institutional history. Karnataka Soaps and Detergents Limited maintains what amounts to a de facto monopoly on the production of soap using pure, authentic natural sandalwood oil, an arrangement that stems directly from the state government's continued exclusive legal control over sandalwood resources within Karnataka under the modern Karnataka Forest Act, itself the direct legal descendant of Tipu Sultan's original royal tree declaration. No private competitor, however well capitalized, can legally establish an equivalent authentic sandalwood soap operation within the state, because no private competitor can legally access the raw sandalwood that only the state controlled forest system is permitted to harvest and sell, a legal arrangement that gives Karnataka's state government direct, continuing commercial benefit from a monopoly structure originally established by a ruler with whom the modern Indian state has, in every other respect, an entirely different political relationship than the one Tipu Sultan held with the British colonial administration that ultimately defeated and succeeded him.

The financial results of this continued monopoly arrangement have been genuinely substantial in recent years, offering direct, contemporary evidence that the underlying commodity, whatever the human and ecological cost documented throughout this book's earlier chapters on sandalwood, remains a significant and reliable source of state revenue. Karnataka Soaps and Detergents Limited's dividend payments to the state government have grown considerably across recent fiscal years, reported at approximately fifty four crore rupees in the 2022 to 2023 fiscal year, expanding to roughly one hundred and eight crore rupees the following year, and reaching approximately one hundred and thirty five crore rupees by October 2025, figures that translate into tens of millions of dollars in direct annual revenue flowing to the Karnataka state treasury from a single state owned enterprise built entirely around the continued exploitation of Tipu Sultan's original royal tree, more than two hundred and thirty years after his 1792 decree first established state ownership over it.

This continued commercial success has not, however, insulated the enterprise from the kind of governance controversy that has repeatedly accompanied concentrated state control over a valuable natural resource throughout this book's preceding chapters, and a specific, well documented episode from recent Karnataka political history illustrates the point with particular clarity. In a scandal that generated substantial regional media coverage, Karnataka's state anti corruption body, the Lokayukta, opened an investigation into alleged irregularities in the company's procurement of raw materials, following a formal complaint filed by the company's own employee union alleging financial losses running into the tens of crores of rupees, and pointing toward wrongdoing in contracts worth several hundred crores in total value. The investigation gained particular political weight after Lokayukta officials raided the residence of the son of a sitting state legislator from the Bharatiya Janata Party who, at the time of the raid, was serving as the chairman of Karnataka Soaps and Detergents Limited, a position from which he resigned within days of his son's arrest, an episode that placed the modern institutional descendant of Tipu Sultan's sandalwood monopoly squarely at the center of a genuine, contemporary state corruption scandal, involving allegations of financial impropriety in the management of the very state controlled resource this book has already documented as sustaining, across more than two centuries, one of the longest running and most economically consequential natural resource monopolies anywhere in South Asian history.

A separate and, in its own way, equally revealing controversy emerged more recently still, when the Karnataka state government's decision to appoint a prominent, pan Indian film actress as brand ambassador for Mysore Sandal Soap triggered a genuine public debate over regional identity and representation, a debate that illustrates just how deeply the soap's brand has become entangled with Kannada regional pride and cultural symbolism, well beyond its purely commercial function as a consumer product. Critics of the appointment argued that selecting a brand ambassador without strong specific ties to Karnataka's own Kannada language film industry represented a symbolic disconnect from the soap's core identity as an emblem of specifically Karnataka heritage, purity, and state pride, a heritage rooted, whether the participants in this contemporary marketing controversy fully recognized it or not, directly in the specific royal monopoly decree Tipu Sultan issued in 1792 to fund his kingdom's defense against advancing British military power. Supporters of the appointment countered that Mysore Sandal Soap, competing today within a national and increasingly global consumer goods marketplace dominated by well resourced multinational brands, required a nationally recognizable ambassador capable of extending its commercial reach well beyond its traditional Karnataka home market. The controversy, whatever its ultimate resolution, demonstrates with unusual clarity a pattern this book has traced from its opening pages in Grasse through its most recent chapters on Bulgaria and Somaliland: a fragrant commodity, once established as a defining feature of a specific regional or national identity, accumulates a form of symbolic and political significance that persists and evolves across generations, well beyond whatever originally utilitarian, revenue generating purpose first justified state control over its production.

The underlying resource constraint that has shaped this entire two century institutional history remains, even now, the central unresolved tension running through Karnataka's sandalwood soap industry. Karnataka Soaps and Detergents Limited depends, for its core product's continued authenticity and market differentiation, on continued access to genuine natural sandalwood oil sourced from state forests that, as this book's earlier chapters documented in considerable detail, suffered catastrophic depletion across the final decades of the twentieth century, with legal production collapsing from roughly three thousand tonnes annually in 1978 to a mere twenty tonnes by 2002, a decline driven substantially by the same underlying pricing distortions and enforcement failures that sustained Veerappan's three decade smuggling career. This resource scarcity has forced the company, in recent years, to supplement its traditional pure natural sandalwood oil sourcing with imported sandalwood and, in certain product lines, synthetic sandalwood fragrance compounds of exactly the type examined in this book's preceding chapter on the broader chemical revolution that transformed twentieth century perfumery, a genuinely significant compromise for a brand whose entire historical identity and commercial differentiation rested on the specific claim of authentic, natural, state controlled sandalwood provenance.

This tension, between a brand whose commercial and cultural value depends fundamentally on authentic natural material sourcing, and a resource base whose sustainable supply has been severely and demonstrably compromised by more than two centuries of the very monopoly control system that brand exists to commercially exploit, captures with unusual precision the central paradox running through this entire book. State control over a scarce, geographically fixed fragrant resource can generate extraordinary and genuinely durable revenue, as Karnataka Soaps and Detergents Limited's recent dividend figures amply demonstrate, sustained across more than two centuries of dramatically different political systems from royal Mysore through British colonial administration to independent Indian statehood. But that same control system, when it prioritizes short term revenue extraction over genuine long term forest sustainability, as Karnataka's sandalwood policy has been repeatedly documented as doing across the twentieth and into the twenty first centuries, ultimately threatens the very resource base upon which its own continued commercial success depends, creating exactly the kind of self undermining institutional logic that recurs, in different specific forms, across nearly every scent trade conflict this book has examined, from the overharvested Boswellia forests of Somaliland to the collapsing musk deer populations of the high Himalaya.

Private cultivation reforms enacted in 2001, discussed in an earlier chapter, offer at least the theoretical prospect of a more sustainable long term supply base for Karnataka's sandalwood soap industry, as private plantations established under the more liberalized post 2001 legal framework gradually approach commercial maturity across the coming decades. Whether Karnataka Soaps and Detergents Limited, as a fundamentally state owned enterprise whose commercial success has for over a century depended on its exclusive relationship with state controlled forest resources, can successfully adapt its business model to incorporate meaningful supply from private growers, a group of suppliers genuinely outside the traditional state monopoly structure the company's entire two century history has been built around, remains a genuinely open institutional question, one that will likely determine whether the specific brand Krishna Raja Wadiyar the Fourth launched in 1918 to solve a wartime export surplus problem can successfully navigate its way through the sustainability crisis its own underlying monopoly structure has, across the intervening century, done so much to help create.

What the modern story of Mysore Sandal Soap ultimately adds to this book's broader argument is a demonstration of just how thoroughly a fragrant commodity monopoly, once established, can become woven into the deep institutional and cultural fabric of a modern state government, surviving not merely the change of political regime that this book has already documented across the transition from Tipu Sultan's kingdom to British colonial rule to independent Karnataka, but also surviving as a genuinely contemporary source of both state revenue and state controversy, generating corruption scandals investigated by modern anti corruption bodies, triggering public debates over regional cultural representation conducted through the thoroughly modern medium of celebrity brand endorsement marketing, and continuing, even now, to depend for its core commercial identity on a natural resource whose sustainable future remains, more than two centuries after a defeated eighteenth century ruler first declared it the property of the crown, genuinely uncertain.

CHAPTER TWELVE

The Last Distillers

Every commodity examined in this book has, at some point across its documented history, encountered a moment when the underlying arithmetic of natural extraction simply stopped working, when the volume of material a forest, a valley, or an ocean could sustainably provide fell permanently behind the volume the global market demanded. Producing a single kilogram of rose oil requires processing roughly five thousand kilograms of fresh rose petals. A kilogram of jasmine absolute requires close to seven million individual jasmine buds, each picked by hand before dawn during a harvest window measured in weeks. Extracting genuine oud oil from agarwood trees requires years of patient cultivation and a naturally occurring fungal infection that cannot be reliably induced at industrial scale. These are not abstractions. They are the specific, physical reasons why every conflict this book has documented, the violence in Mysore's forests, the smuggling networks moving ambergris across a dozen jurisdictions, the poaching that has pushed musk deer toward genuine ecological crisis, ultimately trace back to a single, stubborn fact: nature simply does not produce fragrant materials fast enough, or reliably enough, to meet the scale of demand that centuries of human desire for beautiful scent have generated.

The twenty first century has brought a second wave of technological disruption to this fundamental scarcity problem, one considerably more sophisticated than the nineteenth and twentieth century synthetic chemistry revolution examined earlier in this book, and one whose ultimate effect on the underlying conflicts this book has documented remains, even now, genuinely uncertain. Where the earlier synthetic chemistry revolution worked by identifying a natural scent's key aromatic compounds and then manufacturing chemically identical or closely related molecules from petrochemical feedstocks, a distinct and more recent approach, broadly described as biosynthesis or fermentation based fragrance production, works instead by identifying the actual genetic machinery a plant or other organism uses to produce its characteristic scent, and then transplanting that genetic machinery directly into engineered yeast or bacteria, organisms that can then be cultivated in industrial fermentation vats to produce genuine, molecularly authentic natural fragrance compounds without requiring the original plant, tree, or animal to be grown, harvested, or killed at all.

The specific application of this technology to sandalwood, the single commodity that has occupied more pages of this book than any other, illustrates both the genuine promise and the practical limitations of this new technological approach with particular clarity. The Swiss fragrance house Firmenich, building on research the company began through a partnership with the industrial biotechnology firm Amyris, developed a fermentation based sandalwood alternative marketed under the name Dreamwood, engineered to reproduce santalol, the specific aromatic compound class responsible for sandalwood's distinctive warm, creamy scent, through a fermentation process using natural sugar as its feedstock rather than requiring the thirty to sixty year cultivation cycle, and the corresponding two centuries of monopoly control, violence, and smuggling this book has documented, that authentic Mysore sandalwood extraction has always demanded. A rival German based fragrance company, Symrise, has pursued a parallel biotechnology approach to the same underlying santalol molecule, reflecting genuine, well resourced, competitive industrial investment across multiple major fragrance houses in solving precisely the sandalwood supply crisis this book's second and third chapters documented in such painful historical and human detail.

Rose oil, the commodity whose Bulgarian production history occupied this book's fifth chapter, has received broadly comparable biotechnological attention in recent years. Researchers studying Rosa damascena, the specific damask rose variety that made the Kazanlak and Karlovo valleys famous, have successfully identified specific genes, including ones designated MYB1, CCD1, and PAL in the relevant scientific literature, that govern the biochemical pathways responsible for the rose's distinctive scent profile, and have successfully transferred at least some of this genetic machinery into engineered yeast cultures capable of producing phenylethyl alcohol, one of the key aromatic compounds contributing to authentic rose fragrance. Separate biotechnology approaches using cultured rose plant cells rather than genetically engineered yeast have reported achieving fragrance molecule concentrations up to ten times higher than what conventional field cultivation typically yields, while consuming a documented ninety percent less water than traditional rose farming requires, efficiency gains that, if they continue to scale successfully toward genuine commercial production, could eventually offer at least a partial alternative to the narrow, weather dependent, geographically concentrated harvest system that has defined Bulgaria's Rose Valley industry since the early eighteenth century.

Perhaps the most conceptually striking application of this broader biotechnological approach involves fragrances reconstructed not from currently living plants at all, but from extinct ones, preserved only as dried specimens in herbarium collections. In 2025, a fragrance venture called Future Society, working in collaboration with perfumers from the major fragrance house Givaudan, unveiled a small collection of fragrances built around genetic sequencing extracted directly from preserved botanical specimens, including one scent reconstructing the fragrance of Hibiscadelphus wilderianus, a Hawaiian flowering plant species that has not been documented in the wild since 1912 and is now formally classified as extinct. By extracting whatever fragmentary genetic material survived within decades old, carefully preserved herbarium specimens, and combining that genetic information with engineered yeast fermentation, researchers were able to reconstruct, at least approximately, the specific scent profile of a plant that no living human being now alive has ever actually smelled, a genuinely remarkable technical achievement that nonetheless raises its own set of interesting questions about authenticity, provenance, and what exactly a fragrance built this way is actually claiming to represent.

What all of these developments share, whatever their individual technical differences, is a shared strategic logic that connects them directly back to the deepest argument running through this entire book. Every conflict this book has documented, the two hundred year sandalwood war between Indian state governments and forest bandits, the black markets sustaining an illegal ambergris trade across a dozen jurisdictions, the poaching pressure that has pushed Himalayan musk deer toward genuine ecological crisis, the overtapping concerns now emerging around Somaliland's frankincense producing Boswellia forests, ultimately traces back to the same underlying structural cause: a valuable fragrant material exists in genuinely limited natural supply, concentrated within a specific, geographically constrained region, creating exactly the kind of artificial and natural scarcity that has, across every chapter of this book, proven capable of generating outsized economic and political leverage, smuggling economies, and in the most extreme documented cases, sustained lethal violence. Fermentation based biosynthesis attacks this scarcity at its structural root more directly than even the earlier petrochemical synthetic revolution managed to achieve, because it produces the actual, molecularly authentic natural compound, not merely a chemically similar approximation, without requiring any of the land, any of the multi decade cultivation timelines, or any of the geographic monopoly control that has driven every conflict this book has examined.

Industry figures on the current scale of this transformation suggest a genuinely significant, ongoing structural shift already well underway within the broader fragrance industry, independent of whatever ultimate resolution individual biotechnology ventures like Dreamwood or Future Society's extinct flower project eventually achieve. Current estimates place roughly seventy percent of a typical contemporary perfumer's working material palette as already synthetic in origin, a figure that reflects the cumulative, century and a half long effect of the chemistry revolution examined in an earlier chapter, even before accounting for the newer wave of fermentation based biosynthesis now beginning to supplement, and in some specific product categories potentially replace, both traditional natural harvesting and traditional petrochemical synthesis alike. The scale of contemporary demand driving this shift is itself worth noting explicitly: the global perfume industry has been documented growing at an annual rate variously estimated between fifteen and twenty five percent in recent years, a pace of expansion that natural material supply, constrained by exactly the biological and geographic limitations this book has documented in painstaking detail across its preceding chapters, simply cannot realistically match through conventional cultivation and harvesting methods alone, whatever the underlying commercial or cultural demand for authentic natural provenance among the industry's most prestige conscious luxury consumers.

It would, however, be a significant overstatement to conclude that biotechnology has resolved, or is even close to fully resolving, the underlying conflicts this book has documented, and several genuine, unresolved limitations deserve honest acknowledgment before this book's argument reaches its conclusion. Fermentation based biosynthesis, for all its genuine technical sophistication, has so far proven capable of reproducing individual, specific aromatic compounds with real precision, but has generally struggled to fully replicate the complete, extraordinarily complex chemical profile that a genuine natural essential oil actually contains, the same fundamental limitation that constrained the earlier petrochemical synthetic revolution and that continues to sustain a persistent, prestige driven premium market for authentic natural materials among the world's most demanding luxury perfume houses, exactly the market segment whose continued economic demand has kept every conflict this book has documented genuinely alive and ongoing well into the present day, despite more than a century of advancing synthetic and biosynthetic alternative technology.

The regulatory framework governing international trade in the natural materials this book has examined has evolved considerably since the earliest chapters of this book's story, though evolution has not always translated cleanly into effective enforcement, and this book has documented that gap repeatedly and honestly across its preceding chapters. The Convention on International Trade in Endangered Species, established in 1975 and already discussed in this book's chapters on musk deer and ambergris, has expanded its protective coverage considerably since its original ratification, and contemporary CITES enforcement mechanisms, including expanded international cooperation protocols, improved forensic techniques for identifying trafficked wildlife products, and growing coordination between national customs and wildlife enforcement agencies, represent a genuinely more sophisticated regulatory apparatus than existed when Tipu Sultan first declared sandalwood a royal tree in 1792, or even when the original 1979 CITES musk deer listing first attempted to formally restrict that particular trade. Whether this more sophisticated regulatory apparatus can genuinely close the fundamental economic gap this book has documented repeatedly, between what a black market smuggler can realistically earn from illegal harvest and what a legal, licensed alternative can offer, remains, as this book's chapters on both sandalwood and musk deer have already demonstrated at length, the single most persistent unresolved question running through the entire modern history of scent trade regulation.

Climate change introduces a further, genuinely destabilizing variable into this already complex picture, one that several of the specific commodities this book has examined are already beginning to confront directly. Bulgaria's Rose Valley, whose centuries old prosperity has always depended on a specific, historically reliable combination of mild winter temperatures, adequate spring rainfall during the critical May and June flowering period, and the particular cinnamon colored forest soil chemistry this book's fifth chapter described in some detail, faces genuine emerging uncertainty as shifting regional precipitation and temperature patterns threaten to disrupt growing conditions that Bulgarian rose cultivation has depended upon, largely unchanged, since the early eighteenth century. Somaliland's frankincense producing Boswellia forests face comparable climate driven stress, compounding the overtapping concerns this book's seventh chapter already documented, as shifting rainfall patterns across the broader Horn of Africa region place additional strain on tree populations already under sustained commercial harvesting pressure. Grasse's own historic jasmine and rose growing microclimate, the very foundation of this book's opening chapter, likewise faces long term uncertainty as broader Mediterranean climate patterns continue shifting in ways that may, over coming decades, alter growing conditions that have remained remarkably stable across more than four centuries of continuous cultivation.

What emerges from this survey of the contemporary landscape, taken as a whole, is neither a story of clean technological triumph over centuries of scarcity driven conflict, nor a story of unchanging, permanent violence destined to continue indefinitely in exactly the form this book has documented across its historical chapters. It is instead a genuinely open, still unfolding transition, one in which biotechnology offers real, partial relief from some of the specific scarcity pressures that have driven this book's documented conflicts, even as persistent consumer demand for authentic natural provenance, genuine remaining limitations in biosynthetic technology's ability to fully replicate natural complexity, and the emerging additional pressure of climate change on already stressed natural growing regions together ensure that the underlying economic logic this book has traced from sixteenth century Grasse through twenty first century Karnataka remains, in substantial part, still very much intact.

The specific individuals and institutions this book has examined, the glovemakers of Grasse who first disguised their tannery's stench with jasmine, Tipu Sultan issuing his royal tree decree from a kingdom bracing for renewed war, Jan Pieterszoon Coen ordering the massacre of an entire indigenous population to secure a Dutch nutmeg monopoly, Veerappan and the two state governments his hostage taking briefly brought to a standstill, the Bulgarian rose growers caught within a much larger imperial crisis they had no hand in creating, the frankincense harvesting women of contemporary Somaliland now serving as their families' primary breadwinners, the chemists who broke musk's ancient monopoly with an accidental laboratory discovery aimed originally at explosives, are, each of them, participants in a single continuous story that stretches back across at least five thousand documented years of human history and that shows, on the evidence this book's final chapter has now assembled, no genuine sign of concluding. Human beings have wanted to smell beautiful, and have been willing to pay extraordinary sums, defend extraordinary monopolies, and in the most extreme cases documented across these pages, kill and die, to control the specific, scarce, geographically fixed natural materials capable of producing that beauty, for as long as any written record of human commerce has survived to tell us about it. Whatever combination of fermentation vats, genetically engineered yeast, and reconstructed extinct flower genomes the coming decades bring, the deeper human desire that has driven every single conflict this book has documented shows no evidence whatsoever of fading, and the last distillers, whether they work today with copper cauldrons in the Bulgarian hills or with engineered microorganisms in a Swiss biotechnology laboratory, remain engaged in fundamentally the same ancient project: capturing, however imperfectly, however expensively, and however contested the underlying source material remains, a scent worth wanting badly enough to fight for.

About the Author

Drusilla Nightham is a historian and journalist specializing in the economic history of natural resource trades. This is her first book.

www.ingramcontent.com/pod-product-compliance
Lightning Source LLC
LaVergne TN
LVHW100146061126
851857LV00010B/263